McGraw-Hill Education

Mathematical Reasoning Workbook for the

GED® Test

McGraw-Hill Education

Mathematical Reasoning Workbook for the

GED® Test

McGraw-Hill Education Editors

Contributor: Jouve North America

New York Chicago San Francisco Athens London Madrid
Mexico City Milan New Delhi Singapore Sydney Toronto

1 2 3 4 5 6 7 8 9 10   RHR   19 18 17 16 15 14

ISBN   978-0-07-183183-3
MHID   0-07-183183-5

e-ISBN   978-0-07-183184-0
e-MHID   0-07-183184-3

Library of Congress Control Number 2014940125

GED® is a registered trademark of the American Council on Education (ACE) and administered exclusively by GED Testing Service LLC under license. This content is not endorsed or approved by ACE or GED Testing Service.

Interior design by THINK Book Works
Interior artwork by Cenveo® Publisher Services

McGraw-Hill Education products are available at special quantity discounts to use as premiums and sales promotions or for use in corporate training programs. To contact a representative, please visit the Contact Us pages at www.mhprofessional.com.

Contents

v

Introduction

How to Use This Workbook

This workbook contains practice problems to help you sharpen your mathematical skills in preparation for taking the GED® Mathematical Reasoning test.

Start your mathematics practice by taking the Mathematical Reasoning Pretest at the beginning of this book. It will help you decide which chapters of the workbook will be most valuable to you. You will also see some samples of the special question formats that appear on the actual exam. Take the pretest in a controlled environment, with as few distractions as possible. Use a calculator, and if you want to more closely simulate testing conditions, limit yourself to 90 minutes, although you may prefer taking the test untimed in order to get a chance to think about every problem. When you are done, or when time is up, check your answers in the Answers and Solutions directly following the pretest, where you will find short explanations of a correct approach to each problem. Next, find the problem numbers you answered incorrectly in the Evaluation Chart to identify the chapters on which you need to concentrate.

Each of the twelve chapters in the book consists of an exercise of 50 problems on a different individual topic in mathematics. The number of problems is intended to expose you to the variety of contexts and situations in which various mathematical problems arise. The questions have also been carefully designed to match each of the following:

- the test content specified by the test makers

- the "depth of knowledge" (DOK) levels that the test makers use to measure how well you understand each topic

- the Common Core State Standards (CCSS) that the test makers expect you to have mastered

The exercises are not intended to be timed, but if you find that you are familiar with a topic, you could try timing yourself on a few problems, attempting to correctly work 5 problems in 9 minutes, for example. Answers and Solutions for the problems in the exercises are located directly following the last chapter.

Finally, when you have completed the last exercise, take the Mathematical Reasoning Posttest at the back of this book. This test can help you to reevaluate yourself after practicing in the workbook as much as you feel is necessary. It also contains more samples of the special question formats used on the real exam. Answers and Solutions are located at the end of the posttest, which can help you decide if you are ready to take the GED® Mathematical Reasoning test or if you need further practice.

The GED® Mathematical Reasoning Test

The GED® Mathematical Reasoning test is divided into two parts. Part I consists of 5 questions to be completed without a calculator. A calculator is available for Part II. Once you have started working on Part II, you will not be able to return to Part I. The individual parts are not timed, but the entire test is limited to 90 minutes.

The GED® Mathematical Reasoning test is a computer-based test, which allows for a broad range of item types. There are many multiple-choice items, each of which has four answer choices from which to choose. There are also many technology-based items with formats such as fill-in-the-blank, drop-down, hot spot, and drag-and-drop.

- **Fill-in-the-blank:** These are short-answer items in which a numerical response may be entered directly from the keyboard or in which an expression, equation, or inequality may be entered using an on-screen character selector with mathematical symbols not found on the keyboard.

- **Drop-down:** A list of possible responses is displayed when the response area is clicked with the mouse. These may occur more than once in a sentence or question.

- **Hot spot:** Images on the screen have one or more areas where a response is entered by clicking with the mouse. For example, a line in a coordinate system is entered by clicking the locations of two points on the line.

- **Drag-and-drop:** Small images, words, equations, or other elements are moved around the screen by pointing at them with the mouse, holding the mouse button down, and then releasing the button when the element is positioned over an area on the screen. Such items are used for sorting, classifying, or ordering questions.

About 45 percent of the problems on the test are qualitative, including problems using whole numbers, negative numbers, fractions, decimals, and percentages to answer questions on calculations, conversions, exponents, word problems, rates, ratios, proportions, counting, probability, statistics, data analysis, the Pythagorean theorem, and the perimeter, area, surface area, and volume of geometric objects. These topics are covered in chapters 1–8 of this workbook. The remaining 55 percent of the problems on the test are algebraic, covering algebraic expressions, polynomials, rational expressions, equations, inequalities, graphing, and functions. These topics are covered in chapters 9–12 of this workbook. Due to the nature of mathematics, there will be overlap; for instance, an algebraic expression might be partially expressed with fractions, or an equation might involve using decimals.

Visit http://www.gedtestingservice.com for more about the GED® test.

Mathematical Reasoning

50 questions | **90 minutes**

This pretest is intended to give you an idea of the topics you need to study to pass the GED® Mathematical Reasoning test. Try to work every problem, in a quiet area and with enough time so that you are free from distractions. The usual time allotted for the test is 90 minutes, but it is more important to be sure you get a chance to think about every problem than it is to finish ahead of time.

Answers and solutions for every problem can be found at the end of the pretest.

For questions 1–3, fill in the missing items.

	Decimal	Percent	Fraction
1.	0.03	_____	_____
2.	_____	45%	_____
3.	_____	_____	$\frac{7}{15}$

4. A store reduces the price of a toaster by 25%. The salesperson gives a customer an additional 10% off. What is the total discount the customer is getting, expressed as a percentage?

   A. 1%
   B. 2.5%
   C. 32.5%
   D. 35%

5. If $A > B$, what is the correct relationship for

   $-A$ _____ $-B$? *Write the correct symbol on the line.*

6. Write the equation of a line parallel to $y = 7x + 2$ and passing through the point $(5, 10)$. *Write your answer in the space below.*

7. Convert the fraction $\frac{3}{8}$ to an equivalent fraction with a denominator of 32. *Write your answer in the box.*

8. Solve by factoring: $3x^2 - 5x - 12 = 0$. *Write your answer in the space below.*

9. Which of the lines below is not parallel to $x - 2y = 12$?

   A. $y = -\frac{1}{2}x - 4$
   B. $2x - 4y = 16$
   C. $y = \frac{1}{2}x + 21$
   D. $x - 2y = 8$

For questions 10–12, write your answer in the space provided.

10. Solve for x: $3x + 12 > 2x + 1$.

11. Multiply $(2x - 7)(3x + 1)$.

12. Add $\dfrac{1}{4} + \dfrac{2}{3}$.

13. What is the distance between −4 and 4 on the number line?

    A. 0
    B. −8
    C. 8
    D. 16

14. Arrange in order from least to greatest: $\dfrac{1}{8}, \dfrac{2}{3}, \dfrac{3}{5}, \dfrac{2}{7}, \dfrac{5}{6}$. *Write your answer in the space below.*

15. Given a 6-sided die (one of a pair of dice) that measures 1.75 centimeters on an edge, what is the volume of the die? *Write your answer in the box.*

    ☐ cm³

16. A bowl of colored balls contains 30% red balls, 20% blue balls, and 30% green balls; the rest are white balls. What is the probability of randomly selecting a color other than red on a single draw? *Write your answer in the box.*

    ☐

For questions 17–18, write your answer in the space provided.

17. 25% : 75% :: _____ : 18

18. 3 : 10 :: _____ : 150

19. The ratio 5:7 is the same as

    A. 35
    B. $\dfrac{5}{7}$
    C. $\dfrac{7}{5}$
    D. 0.625

For questions 20–21, write your answer in the space provided.

20. Suzy has made a mistake and added 4 teaspoons of baking powder to 5 cups of flour in a recipe that calls for 3 teaspoons of baking soda to 5 cups of flour. In order to not waste the entire batch, she has decided to add flour to get the proper proportion of baking powder to flour. How much flour should she add?

21. Subtract $-7x + 2$ from $4x + 7$.

22. A group of 16 adults, 9 of whom are men, have placed their names on slips of paper in a large bowl. What is the probability of selecting three women's names in a row? *Write your answer in the box.*

    ☐

23. Which of the following is (are) NOT function(s)?

A.
x	1	2	5	−1	−5
y	2	3	9	7	2

B.
x	−2	−1	0	1	2
y	4	4	4	4	4

C.
x	−1	2	−1	4	−1
y	2	4	3	11	2

D.
x	−2	−1	0	−1	−2
y	15	7	0	7	15

For questions 24–40, write your answer in the space provided.

24. A business owner adds 45% to the price of an item to cover operating costs and profit margin. What is the selling price of an item that costs the owner $120?

25. What is the value of $2x^2 + 3y^3$ when $x = 3.5$ and $y = 2.25$?

26. For what integer values of x is $x > 4$ true?

27. Starting at −14 on the number line, in which direction must you go, left or right, to find −11?

28. If $y = \sqrt{x - 2}$, then for what values of x is y a real number?

29. What is the area of a triangle with a base of 15 and a height of 6?

30. What is the slope of a line perpendicular to $3x + 4y = 13$?

31. What is the perimeter of a rectangular field that measures 660 feet by 330 feet?

32. Reduce to lowest terms: $\dfrac{x^5}{x^3}$.

33. How many cubic centimeters can a tin can hold if it is 11.0 centimeters high and its top is 7.4 centimeters in diameter?

34. Multiply 3.45 by 0.765 by 34.505.

35. If $f(x) = 5x^2 - 7x + 4$, what is $f(-2)$?

36. $x^{-3} =$ _____

37. Add $45.05 + 1.007 + 3.0754 + 0.001$.

38. Graph $3x - 5y = -10$.

39. Simplify $\dfrac{6x^2 + 8x}{2x^2}$.

40. Simplify $\sqrt[4]{162}$.

41. Is this the graph of a function? Check ____ Yes or ____ No.

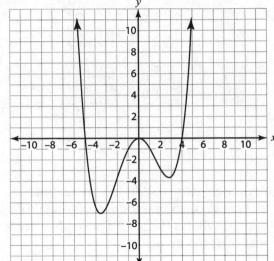

42. Can you divide $\dfrac{y^4}{x^2}$? Check ____ Yes or ____ No.

43. Multiply $(x + 2)^2$.
    A. $x^2 + 4$
    B. $4x^2$
    C. $x^2 + 2x + 4$
    D. $x^2 + 4x + 4$

44. If housing prices have increased by 17% since last year, what was the old price of a house that today sells for $185,000? *Write your answer in the box.*

$ [   ]

For questions 45–50, write your answer in the space provided.

45. Subtract $\dfrac{2x+2}{4y} - \dfrac{3x-7}{2x}$.

46. Given the equation $y = 3x + 4$, what are the slope and y intercept?

47. A bag has 6 red marbles and 12 blue marbles. A marble is drawn from the bag at random. What is the probability that it is blue?

48. What are the mean, median, and mode of the data set {5, 3, 6, 4, 6, 2, 8, 2, 6, 3, 6, 9, 1, 4, 7}?

49. Solve $x^2 - 5x - 6 = 0$.

50. Solve $-2x + 17 > 11$.

THIS IS THE END OF THE MATHEMATICAL REASONING PRETEST.

ANSWERS AND SOLUTIONS BEGIN ON THE NEXT PAGE.

Answers and Solutions

	Decimal	Percent	Fraction
1.	0.03	3%	$\dfrac{3}{100}$
2.	0.45	45%	$\dfrac{9}{20}$
3.	0.467	46.7%	$\dfrac{7}{15}$

4. **C** — The discounts are stacked. The first 25% discount cuts the cost down to 75%. The second discount of 10% applies to the reduced price and is worth only 7.5% of the original price. Combined, the two discounts add up to 32.5% off the original price.

5. **$-A < -B$** — Multiplying both sides of an inequality by a negative number changes the direction of the inequality symbol.

6. **$y = 7x - 25$** — To be parallel, the slopes of the two lines need to be equal, so the new line is $y = 7x + b$. Since all points on a line satisfy the equation, we can substitute 5 for x and 10 for y to get $10 = 7(5) + b$ and solve to find b: $10 = 35 + b \rightarrow 10 - 35 = b \rightarrow -25 = b$. With $b = -25$, the equation becomes $y = 7x - 25$.

7. **$\dfrac{12}{32}$** — The denominator and numerator are both multiplied by 4.

8. **$x = -\dfrac{4}{3}$ or $x = 3$** — $(3x + 4)(x - 3) = 0 \rightarrow$
$3x + 4 = 0$ or $x - 3 = 0 \rightarrow$
$3x = -4$ or $x = 3 \rightarrow$
$x = -\dfrac{4}{3}$ or $x = 3$

Solving both for x gives the answer.

9. **A** — Solving the equation in the question and the equations in choices B and D for y all produce $y = \dfrac{1}{2}x + b$ for different values of b, but they all have a slope $m = \dfrac{1}{2}$, as does choice C. The slope in choice A is $-\dfrac{1}{2}$.

10. **$x > -11$** — $3x + 12 - 2x > 2x + 1 - 2x \rightarrow$
$x + 12 > 1 \rightarrow$
$x + 12 - 12 > 1 - 12 \rightarrow x > -11$

11. **$6x^2 - 19x - 7$**
$2x \cdot 3x + 2x \cdot 1 - 7 \cdot 3x - 7 \cdot 1 =$
$6x^2 + 2x - 21x - 7 = 6x^2 - 19x - 7$

12. **$\dfrac{11}{12}$** — $\dfrac{1}{4} \cdot \dfrac{3}{3} + \dfrac{2}{3} \cdot \dfrac{4}{4} = \dfrac{3}{12} + \dfrac{8}{12} = \dfrac{11}{12}$

13. **C** — distance $= |-4 - 4| = |-8| = 8$

14. **$\dfrac{1}{8}, \dfrac{2}{7}, \dfrac{3}{5}, \dfrac{2}{3}, \dfrac{5}{6}$**

15. **5.36 cm^3** — $V = (1.75)^3 = 5.359375 \approx 5.36$

16. **70%** — $100\% - 30\% = 70\%$

17. **6** — $\dfrac{0.25}{0.75} = \dfrac{n}{18} \rightarrow 18 \cdot \dfrac{0.25}{0.75} = 18 \cdot \dfrac{n}{18}$
$\rightarrow 18 \cdot \dfrac{1}{3} = n \rightarrow 6 = n$

18. **45** — $\dfrac{3}{10} = \dfrac{n}{150} \rightarrow 150 \cdot \dfrac{3}{10} = 150 \cdot \dfrac{n}{150}$
$\rightarrow 15 \cdot 3 = n \rightarrow 45 = n$

19. **B**

20. $1\frac{2}{3}$ **cups** $\frac{3}{5} = \frac{4}{n} \rightarrow 5n \cdot \frac{3}{5} = 5n \cdot \frac{4}{n} \rightarrow$

$3n = 20 \rightarrow n = \frac{20}{3} = 6\frac{2}{3}$, and

$6\frac{2}{3} - 5 = 1\frac{2}{3}$

21. **11x + 5**   The subtraction must be set up as $4x + 7 - (-7x + 2)$. Change the signs of the second polynomial and add:

$4x + 7 + 7x - 2 = 11x + 5$

22. **6.25%**   Each time a female name is drawn, the number of available names and the number of female names decrease by 1. Each pick is independent, so the probabilities for the three picks are multiplied:

$\frac{7}{16} \cdot \frac{6}{15} \cdot \frac{5}{14} = \frac{210}{3360} = \frac{1}{16} = 0.0625$

23. **C**   Only C violates the definition of function: "for every x, there should be no more than one value of y."

24. **$174**   Markup $= 0.45 \cdot 120 = 54$, selling price $= 120 + 54 = 174$

25. **58.67** $2 \cdot 3.5^2 + 3 \cdot 2.25^3 = 2 \cdot 12.25 + 3 \cdot 11.390625 = 24.5 + 34.171875 = 58.671875$

26. **5,6,7,…**

27. **right**

28. **x ≥ 2**   The quantity beneath the radical sign must be nonnegative. Solving $x - 2 \geq 0$ (add 2 to both sides) gives the answer.

29. **45** $A = \frac{1}{2}bh = \frac{1}{2} \cdot 15 \cdot 6 = \frac{1}{2} \cdot 90 = 45$

30. $\frac{4}{3}$ Solve the given equation for y to find the slope of the given line:

$3x + 4y = 13 \rightarrow 3x + 4y - 3x =$

$13 - 3x \rightarrow 4y = -3x + 13 \rightarrow$

$\frac{4y}{4} = \frac{-3x + 13}{4} \rightarrow y = -\frac{3}{4}x + \frac{13}{4}$,

so $m = -\frac{3}{4}$.

A perpendicular line has a slope that is the negative reciprocal.

31. **1980 ft** $p = 2l + 2h = 2 \cdot 660 + 2 \cdot 330 = 1320 + 660 = 1980$

32. x^2 $x^{5-3} = x^2$

33. **473 cm³** $r = \frac{7.4}{2} = 3.7 \; V = \pi r^2 h = \pi \cdot 3.7^2 \cdot 11 = 3.14 \cdot 13.69 \cdot 11 \approx 473$

34. **91.06732125**

35. **38** $f(-2) = 5(-2)^2 - 7(-2) + 4 = 5 \cdot 4 + 14 + 4 = 20 + 18 = 38$

36. $\frac{1}{x^3}$

37. **49.1334**

38.

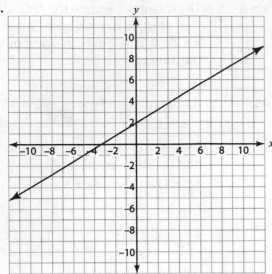

39. $\dfrac{3x+4}{x}$ $\quad \dfrac{6x^2+8x}{2x^2} = \dfrac{(2x)(3x+4)}{(2x)(x)} = \dfrac{3x+4}{x}$

40. $3\sqrt[4]{2}$ $\quad \sqrt[4]{162} = \sqrt[4]{3\cdot3\cdot3\cdot3\cdot2} =$
$\sqrt[4]{3^4}\cdot\sqrt[4]{2} = 3\sqrt[4]{2}$

41. **Yes** Every vertical line crosses the graph no more than once.

42. **No** The variables must be the same.

43. **D** $(x+2)(x+2) = x\cdot x + 2x + 2x +$
$2\cdot2 = x^2 + 4x + 4$

44. **$158,120** Today's price is 117%, or 1.17 times the original. Divide today's price by 1.17 to get $158,120.

45. $\dfrac{x^2 + x - 3xy + 7y}{2xy}$

The least common denominator is $4xy$.

$\dfrac{x}{x}\cdot\dfrac{2x+2}{4y} - \dfrac{2y}{2y}\cdot\dfrac{3x-7}{2x} =$

$\dfrac{2x^2+2x}{4xy} - \dfrac{6xy-14y}{4xy} =$

$\dfrac{2x^2+2x-6xy+14y}{8xy} = \dfrac{x^2+x-3xy+7y}{2xy}$

46. **$m = 3, b = 4$**

The equation is in slope-intercept form, $y = mx + b$.

47. $\dfrac{2}{3}$ For a blue marble, the probability is $\dfrac{12}{18}$, or $\dfrac{2}{3}$.

48. **mean = 4.8, mode = 6, median = 5**

mean $= \dfrac{5+3+6+4+6+2+8+2+6+3+6+9+1+4+7}{15}$

$= \dfrac{72}{15} = 4.8$

sorted data: {1, 2, 2, 3, 3, 4, 4, 5, 6, 6, 6, 6, 7, 8, 9}

mode $= 6$

median $= 5$

49. **6, –1** $(x-6)(x+1) = 0 \rightarrow x - 6 = 0$ or
$x + 1 = 0 \rightarrow x = 6$ or $x = -1$

50. **$x < 3$** $-2x + 17 > 11 \rightarrow -2x > -6 \rightarrow$
$x < 3$

Evaluation Chart

Circle the item number of each problem you missed. To the right of the item numbers, you will find the chapters that cover the skills you need to solve the problems. More problem numbers circled in any row means more attention is needed to sharpen those skills for the GED® test.

Item Numbers	Chapter
13, 27	1. Whole Numbers and Integers
32, 36, 40, 42	2. Exponents, Roots, and Properties of Numbers
1, 2, 3, 7, 12, 14	3. Fractions and Operations
1, 2, 3, 34, 37	4. Decimal Numbers and Operations
17, 18, 19, 20	5. Ratios, Rates, and Proportions
1, 2, 3, 4, 24, 44	6. Percents and Applications
16, 22, ,47, 48	7. Probability and Statistics
15, 29, 31, 33	8. Geometry
11, 21, 25, 39, 43, 45	9. Polynomial and Rational Expressions
5, 8, 10, 26, 49, 50	10. Solving Equations and Inequalities
6, 9, 30, 38, 46	11. Graphing Equations
23, 28, 35, 41	12. Functions

Calculators and the GED® Mathematical Reasoning Test

An on-screen calculator is available for Part II of the GED® Mathematical Reasoning test. It is also available on some of the other test sections, such as the Science section. The calculator is the computer version of Texas Instrument's TI-30XS MultiView. On the screen, the calculator looks like the physical model of the calculator, and it functions in the same manner. You will need only the same functionality as on most basic calculators: addition, subtraction, multiplication, division, and square root. Being aware of some of the other calculator features and being able to use them efficiently may speed up your response time and help you complete the test in the allotted time. The other features you may find useful are the change sign key, the reciprocal function, squaring button, raise-to-a-power button, parentheses, root button, and others. A complete explanation of the full functionality is beyond the scope of the workbook, but here are some pointers:

- Use the change sign key to enter negative numbers. The key is labeled (–) and is different from the subtraction key, which is grouped with the other operation keys.

- Use the reciprocal button, labeled x^{-1}, if you realize you computed a fraction with the numerator and denominator interchanged. This will save you the effort of recalculating the entire fraction.

- Use the raise-to-a-power button, labeled ∧, to compute a number raised to a power. This will save time by not having to reenter a number when raising it to a power; it will also decrease the chance of entering the number incorrectly.

- Use the parentheses to carry out mixed operations without recording intermediate results. The squaring button is a shortcut to raising a number to the second power. It immediately squares the number in the display.

- Use the root button to find decimal approximations of square roots. Other roots may be approximated by using the shifted power key.

Visit http://www.atomiclearning.com/ti30xs for more information about using the calculator, including instructions on some of the advanced features.

CHAPTER 1

Whole Numbers and Integers

Directions: Answer the following questions. For multiple-choice questions, choose the best answer. For other questions, write your answer in the space provided below the question. Answers begin on page 87.

1. Plot the number 47 on the number line.

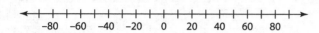

2. Plot the number −25 on the number line.

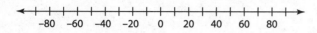

3. Place the correct symbol, < or >, between the

   numbers: −258 _____ 95

4. Place the correct symbol, < or >, between the

   numbers: −47 _____ −44

5. Place the correct symbol, < or >, between the

   numbers: 54 _____ −128

6. What is the opposite of −5, simplified?

   A. −(−5)
   B. $\frac{1}{5}$
   C. $-\frac{1}{5}$
   D. 5

7. What is the simplified form of the opposite of the opposite of 12?

   A. −(−12)
   B. 12
   C. $\frac{1}{12}$
   D. $-\frac{1}{12}$

8. What is |−42|, simplified?

   A. 42
   B. (−42)
   C. −42
   D. |42|

9. What is the absolute value of 7?

   A. |7|
   B. −7
   C. (7)
   D. 7

10. Which quadrant has positive *x* values and negative *y* values?

    A. QI
    B. QII
    C. QIII
    D. QIV

11. Which quadrant has negative *x* values and negative *y* values?

    A. QI
    B. QII
    C. QIII
    D. QIV

12. Which point is the reflection of (−4, 7) in the *x*-axis?

    A. (−4, −7)
    B. (4, −7)
    C. (7, −4)
    D. (−7, 4)

13. Which point is the reflection of (0, −2) in the *x*-axis?

    A. (2, 0)
    B. (0, 2)
    C. (−2, 0)
    D. (0, −2)

14. Which point is the reflection of (2, –5) in the y-axis?

    A. (–2, 5)
    B. (5, –2)
    C. (–5, 2)
    D. (–2, –5)

15. Which point is the reflection of (0, –3) in the y-axis?

    A. (–3, 0)
    B. (3, 0)
    C. (0, –3)
    D. (0, 3)

16. In the diagram, which point has coordinates (–3, 2)?

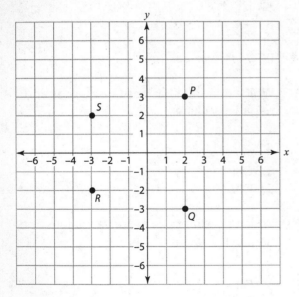

    A. P
    B. Q
    C. R
    D. S

17. In the diagram, which point has coordinates (4, –5)?

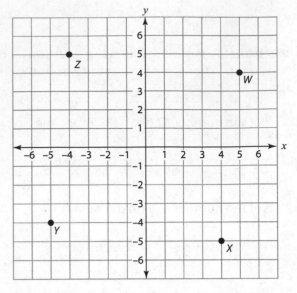

    A. W
    B. X
    C. Y
    D. Z

18. Which statement is true?

    A. –3 < –7
    B. –3 is to the right of –7 of the number line.
    C. |–3| > |–7|
    D. –3 is to the left of –7 on the number line.

19. Death Valley in California has an elevation of –282 feet. The Dead Sea in the Middle East has an elevation of –1360 feet. Which of the following must be true?

    A. The Dead Sea is drier than Death Valley.
    B. Death Valley is closer to sea level.
    C. There are heavier rocks in the Dead Sea.
    D. Death Valley is hotter than the Dead Sea.

20. The absolute value expression |–7| represents

    A. the distance from 7 to –7.
    B. the distance from 7 to 0.
    C. the distance from –7 to 7.
    D. the distance from –7 to 0.

21. What is the geometric meaning of −5 < −2?

    A. −2 is not as negative as −5.
    B. −5 is to the left of −2 on the number line.
    C. −5 is smaller than −2.
    D. −2 is to the right of −5 on the number line.

22. Albert has a bank balance of −65 dollars. George has a balance of −44 dollars. Zoe's balance is −7 dollars; Pat's balance is −82 dollars. Who owes more money to the bank?

    A. Albert
    B. George
    C. Zoe
    D. Pat

23. What is the greatest common factor of 42 and 36?

    A. 4
    B. 6
    C. 7
    D. 9

24. What is the least common multiple of 6 and 9?

    A. 9
    B. 18
    C. 36
    D. 54

25. Which situation describes quantities combining to make 0?

    A. An account overdrawn by $1367 receives a payroll deposit of $756 and a tax refund deposit of $621.
    B. 5 people chip in $17 each to help settle a friend's $85 electricity bill.
    C. A person contributes $15 to pay for his share of a $60 dinner bill; his 4 companions all generously do the same.
    D. Oil leaks out of a full 75,000-gallon tank at the rate of 1500 gallons each day for 7 weeks before someone notices.

26. On a number line, where is the number −2 + (−7)?

    A. 7 units to the right of −2
    B. −7 units to the left of −2
    C. −7 units to the right of −2
    D. 7 units to the left of −2

27. Which number line shows that a number and its opposite have a sum of 0?

    A.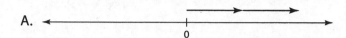

    B.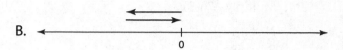

    C.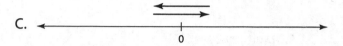

    D.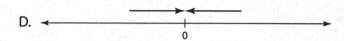

28. Compute 3 − 7.

    A. −10
    B. −4
    C. 4
    D. 10

29. Compute 5 − (−6).

    A. −11
    B. −1
    C. 1
    D. 11

30. Add 7 + (−5) + (−9).

    A. −7
    B. −11
    C. −21
    D. −9

31. Compute −3 − (−8) + (−4) − 5.

    A. −15
    B. −10
    C. −4
    D. 4

32. Add −9 + 3 + (−4).

    A. 2
    B. −2
    C. −10
    D. −16

33. Compute −8 − (−10) − 5.

    A. −3
    B. −23
    C. −7
    D. 3

34. Multiply −7(−9).

    A. −16
    B. −63
    C. 63
    D. 16

35. Multiply 2(−4)(−1).

    A. −8
    B. 8
    C. 7
    D. −3

36. Divide −32 ÷ 8.

    A. −2
    B. 4
    C. −4
    D. 2

37. Divide 42 ÷ (−6).

    A. −7
    B. 36
    C. −36
    D. 7

38. Divide −72 ÷ (−9).

    A. 8
    B. −63
    C. −81
    D. −8

39. Which of the following is NOT equal to −5?

    A. −20 ÷ 4
    B. 20 ÷ (−4)
    C. −20 ÷ (−4)
    D. −(20 ÷ 4)

40. Which expression represents the distance between −5 and 6?

    A. |−5| + |6|
    B. |−5 + 6|
    C. |−5| − |6|
    D. |−5 − 6|

41. Plot and label the points

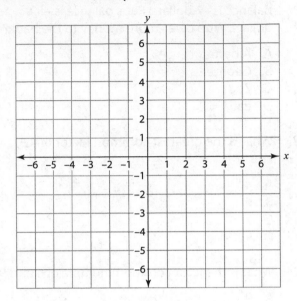

    A (1, −5), B (−2, −3), C (−5, 1)

42. A rocket is about to launch. At T:−52 seconds the guidance system starts its final automatic test. The test is over at T:−17 seconds. How long did the test take?

    A. 49 seconds
    B. 45 seconds
    C. 35 seconds
    D. 39 seconds

43. Which of the following is undefined?

    A. $\dfrac{-2 + 2}{8 + (-4)}$

    B. $\dfrac{5 + (-2)}{-7 + 7}$

    C. $\dfrac{4 - (-1)}{6 - 3}$

    D. $\dfrac{-3 + (-1)}{4 - (-6)}$

44. Arrange these numbers in order from smallest to largest:

    −15, −20, 13, −2, −8, 6, 0

45. What is the distance between −7 and 6 on the number line?

    A. −13
    B. −1
    C. 1
    D. 13

46. What is −0?

47. Which addition problem is shown by the number line?

    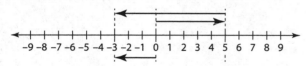

    A. −3 + (−8) = 5
    B. −3 + 5 = −8
    C. 5 + (−8) = −3
    D. −3 + (−5) = −8

48. Which subtraction problem is shown by the number line?

    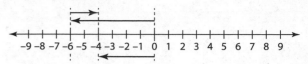

    A. −6 − (−2) = −4
    B. 2 − 6 = −4
    C. −2 − 4 = −6
    D. −4 − 2 = −6

49. Frank hears that the average temperature at a science station in Antarctica one winter is −40°C. He knows he can change the Celsius temperature into Fahrenheit by multiplying the given temperature by 9, adding 160, and then dividing by 5. What temperature should Frank come up with?

    A. −104°F
    B. −40°F
    C. 40°F
    D. 104°F

50. Compute −7(−5) − 4(−8 − 6) ÷ (−2).

    A. −217
    B. 63
    C. 31
    D. 7

CHAPTER 2

Exponents, Roots, and Properties of Numbers

Directions: Choose the best answer to each of the following questions. Answers begin on page 88.

1. Which is the same as $5 \cdot 5 \cdot 5 \cdot 5 \cdot 5 \cdot 5 \cdot 5 \cdot 5 \cdot 5$?

   A. $9 \cdot 5$
   B. $5 \cdot 9$
   C. 5^9
   D. 9^5

2. Rewrite 7^3 as repeated multiplication.

   A. $3 \cdot 3 \cdot 3 \cdot 3 \cdot 3 \cdot 3 \cdot 3$
   B. $7 \cdot 7 \cdot 7$
   C. 2187
   D. 343

3. Rewrite $2 \cdot 2 \cdot 2 \cdot 2 \cdot 2$ with an exponent.

   A. 2^5
   B. 5^2
   C. 32
   D. 10

4. Compute 4^3.

   A. 12
   B. 81
   C. 64
   D. 256

5. Which number is the base in the expression $8 \cdot 3^6$?

   A. 3
   B. 6
   C. 8
   D. 3^6

6. Evaluate 5^3.

   A. 723
   B. 625
   C. 125
   D. 15

7. Which expression is equivalent to $9^5 \cdot 9^3$?

   A. 9^{15}
   B. 81^8
   C. 81^{15}
   D. 9^8

8. Which expression is equivalent to $4^6 \cdot 2^6$?

   A. 6^{36}
   B. 8^{12}
   C. 6^{12}
   D. 8^6

9. Which expression is equivalent to $2^5 \cdot 3^5 \cdot 6^7$?

   A. 6^{12}
   B. 36^{12}
   C. 36^{175}
   D. 11^{12}

10. Simplify $7^3 \cdot 7^2 \cdot 7^5$.

    A. 7^{30}
    B. 7^{10}
    C. 343^{30}
    D. 343^{10}

11. Simplify $2^3 \cdot 4^3 \cdot 5^3$.

    A. 40^9
    B. 11^{27}
    C. 40^3
    D. 11^9

12. What is 12^0?

    A. 0
    B. 1
    C. 12
    D. 120

13. Simplify $(5^3)^4$.

   A. 5^7
   B. 5^{64}
   C. 5^{81}
   D. 5^{12}

14. What is 12^1?

   A. 0
   B. 1
   C. 12
   D. 121

15. Simplify $3 \cdot 3^3$.

   A. 9^3
   B. 3^4
   C. 3^3
   D. 9^4

16. Simplify $6^5(6^2)^3$.

   A. 6^{11}
   B. 6^{10}
   C. 36^{10}
   D. 36^{11}

17. Simplify $(3^5)^2(3^4)^3$.

   A. 3^{120}
   B. 3^{14}
   C. 3^{49}
   D. 3^{22}

18. Simplify 5^{-2}.

   A. $\dfrac{1}{25}$
   B. -10
   C. -25
   D. $\dfrac{1}{10}$

19. Simplify $(2^{-3})^2$.

   A. 36
   B. $\dfrac{1}{32}$
   C. $\dfrac{1}{64}$
   D. -12

20. Rewrite $(5^{-2})^{-4}$.

   A. $\dfrac{1}{5^8}$
   B. 5^8
   C. 400
   D. 10,000

21. Simplify 10^5.

   A. 10,000
   B. 100,000
   C. 50,000
   D. 500,000

22. What is 1^7?

   A. 7
   B. -7
   C. 0
   D. 1

23. Simplify $24 \cdot 2^{-9}$.

   A. $\dfrac{1}{32}$
   B. $\dfrac{1}{10}$
   C. -10
   D. -32

24. Simplify $\dfrac{3^7}{3^5}$.

   A. 9
   B. $\dfrac{1}{9}$
   C. 6
   D. $\dfrac{1}{6}$

25. Simplify $\dfrac{5^3}{5^6}$.

   A. $\dfrac{1}{2}$
   B. $\dfrac{1}{15}$
   C. $\dfrac{1}{125}$
   D. $\dfrac{1}{243}$

26. What is 10^{-2}?

    A. $-\dfrac{1}{100}$

    B. $\dfrac{1}{100}$

    C. -100

    D. 100

27. What is 0^{19}?

    A. 0
    B. 1
    C. 19
    D. -19

28. Simplify $\left(\dfrac{7}{8}\right)^5$.

    A. $\dfrac{35}{40}$

    B. $\dfrac{5^7}{5^8}$

    C. $\dfrac{1}{5}$

    D. $\dfrac{7^5}{8^5}$

29. Evaluate $\left(\dfrac{2}{3}\right)^4$.

    A. $\dfrac{16}{12}$

    B. $\dfrac{16}{81}$

    C. $\dfrac{8}{12}$

    D. $\dfrac{32}{243}$

30. Compute $2^6 \cdot 5^6$.

    A. 360
    B. 60
    C. $1,000,000$
    D. 420

31. Which expression is equivalent to $(5^4 \cdot 7^9)^3$?

    A. $15^7 \cdot 21^{12}$
    B. $15^4 \cdot 21^9$
    C. $5^7 \cdot 7^{12}$
    D. $5^{12} \cdot 7^{27}$

32. Evaluate $100^{\frac{1}{2}}$.

    A. 50
    B. 10
    C. $\dfrac{1}{200}$

    D. $\dfrac{1}{10,000}$

33. Evaluate $8^{\frac{1}{3}}$.

    A. 2

    B. $\dfrac{8}{3}$

    C. $\dfrac{1}{24}$

    D. 512

34. Evaluate $25^{-\frac{1}{2}}$.

    A. $-\dfrac{25}{2}$

    B. $\dfrac{1}{625}$

    C. $\dfrac{1}{5}$

    D. -625

35. Evaluate $1000^{-\frac{1}{3}}$.

    A. -3000

    B. $\dfrac{1}{10}$

    C. $-\dfrac{1000}{3}$

    D. 3000

36. Compute $4^{2^{-1}}$.

    A. 2
    B. 16
    C. -16
    D. -2

37. Write $7^{\frac{1}{2}}$ as a radical.

    A. $\dfrac{7}{2}$

    B. $3\dfrac{1}{2}$

    C. $7\sqrt{2}$

    D. $\sqrt{7}$

38. Write $\sqrt[3]{9}$ as an expression with an exponent.

    A. $(\sqrt[3]{9})^1$

    B. $9^{\frac{1}{3}}$

    C. 3^1

    D. 9^3

39. Write $\sqrt{6}$ as an expression with an exponent.

    A. $3^{\frac{1}{2}}$

    B. 3^1

    C. $6^{\frac{1}{2}}$

    D. $\sqrt{6}^1$

40. Write $4^{\frac{1}{3}}$ as a radical.

    A. $\sqrt[3]{4}$

    B. 2

    C. $\sqrt{4}$

    D. $\sqrt[4]{3}$

41. What is $\sqrt{81}$?

    A. 18

    B. 3

    C. 9

    D. 11

42. What is $\sqrt{36}$?

    A. 18

    B. 6

    C. 3

    D. 72

43. What is $\sqrt[3]{64}$?

    A. 21

    B. 8

    C. 6

    D. 4

44. What is $\sqrt[3]{27}$?

    A. 3

    B. 9

    C. 6

    D. 2

45. Which expression is the same as 54 – 30?

    A. 6(9 – 6)

    B. 6(9 + 6)

    C. 6(9 + 5)

    D. 6(9 – 5)

46. Which of the following is equivalent to 5(7 + 2)?

    A. 35 + 10

    B. 12 + 7

    C. 35 – 10

    D. 12 – 7

47. Which is the same as 3(9 – 5)?

    A. 12 – 8

    B. 27 + 15

    C. 27 – 15

    D. 12 + 8

48. Which expression is the same as 64 + 28?

    A. 20(44 + 8)

    B. 4(16 + 7)

    C. 14(40 + 14)

    D. 8(8 + 3)

49. Select the expression equivalent to 2(3 + 5 – 4).

    A. 5 + 1

    B. 6 + 1

    C. 5 + 7 – 6

    D. 6 + 10 – 8

50. Which expression is the same as –6(8 + 3)?

    A. –48 – 18

    B. –48 + 18

    C. 48 – 18

    D. 48 + 18

CHAPTER 3

Fractions and Operations

Directions: Answer the following questions. For multiple-choice questions, choose the best answer. For other questions, write your answer in the space below the question. Answers begin on page 90.

1. Eli's daughter had a birthday party at Molly Mouse's Pizza Planet. There were two tables of girls. The girls left to play the games and Eli saw that one table had left $\frac{1}{2}$ of a pie and the other had left $\frac{2}{3}$ of a pie. Eli added the two and came up with one full pie and one piece left over. What is the smallest number of pieces that each pie was cut into?

2. Perry's Used Cars gives $\frac{1}{8}$ of the price of a car as commission to its sales force. The members of the sales force share equally in the commission. If there are 6 people selling cars, how much will each get from a car that sells for $7100?

3. A company claims its soap is $99\frac{44}{100}$ percent pure. What is $\frac{44}{100}$ reduced to its lowest form?

4. Laura runs a food bank. On Monday she gave away $\frac{1}{4}$ of her stock of flour. On Tuesday she gave away $\frac{1}{3}$ of what was left from Monday. On Wednesday she gave away $\frac{1}{2}$ of what was left from Tuesday. If she started with 1000 pounds of flour, how much was left by the end of Wednesday?

5. $\frac{1}{3} \div \frac{5}{3} = ?$

A. $\frac{5}{9}$

B. 5

C. $\frac{9}{5}$

D. $\frac{1}{5}$

6. Toni had a backlog of work to do. On Monday she did $\frac{1}{4}$ of the backlog. If on Tuesday she does the same amount of work (e.g., processes the exact same number of files), what part of the backlog will be left?

7. Lonnie announces a sale of $\frac{1}{3}$ off all merchandise and puts special sale tags on every item. Toward the end of the sale, she decides to give customers an additional $\frac{1}{3}$ off the marked-down prices. What is the total discount?

   A. $\frac{1}{9}$ of the original price

   B. $\frac{2}{3}$ of the original price

   C. $\frac{5}{9}$ of the original price

   D. $\frac{4}{9}$ of the original price

8. Add $1\frac{5}{8}$ and $4\frac{4}{5}$.

9. Saul the butcher mixes $15\frac{3}{4}$ pounds of beef and $12\frac{3}{8}$ pounds of pork together to make sausage. How many pounds of sausage will he get from these two meats?

10. Julie usually puts $23\frac{1}{4}$ pounds of flour in her cookie recipe. But this time she is short of another ingredient and must cut her flour by $7\frac{3}{5}$ pounds. How much flour will she put in the recipe?

11. Tomasz multiplied $\frac{3}{4}$ by $1\frac{1}{5}$ and got $\frac{3}{4}$ for an answer. Did he do something wrong?

   A. No, that is the correct answer.
   B. Yes, he did not change the mixed number to an improper fraction.
   C. Yes, he forgot to invert the second fraction.
   D. Yes, he did not add 1 when he converted the mixed number to an improper fraction (he multiplied $\frac{3}{4}$ by $\frac{5}{5}$ rather than by $\frac{6}{5}$).

12. In one town are 25 drivers under the age of 21. There are a total of 225 drivers in town. What is the fraction of drivers under 21?

   A. $\frac{1}{10}$

   B. $\frac{1}{9}$

   C. $\frac{1}{8}$

   D. $\frac{1}{5}$

13. Aram has $6\frac{1}{2}$ pounds of dry grout for tiling his shower floor. If he takes away $3\frac{7}{8}$ pounds for the first batch of grout, how much does he have left?

14. Sandi has brewed 55 ounces of iced tea. How many full glasses of tea can be filled if it takes $7\frac{3}{4}$ ounces of tea to fill each glass?

15. Cal must cut 5 pieces of lumber, each measuring $11\frac{9}{16}$ inches, from an 8-foot board. If Cal's saw blade is $\frac{1}{8}$ inch wide (i.e., $\frac{1}{8}$ inch of wood is lost on every cut), how much of the board will be left after Cal gets his five pieces?

16. Recently, the number of Americans under age 18 with student loans has increased from $\frac{14}{100}$ to $\frac{1}{5}$. Express the difference as a fraction reduced to its lowest terms.

17. What is $\frac{11}{45}$ multiplied by its reciprocal?

18. What is $\frac{3}{4}$ expressed in 64ths?

19. Which of the following is exactly equal to 1?

    A. the reciprocal of $\frac{3}{15}$

    B. the opposite of $\frac{3}{15}$ times $\frac{3}{15}$

    C. $\frac{15}{3}$ divided by $\frac{15}{3}$

    D. none of these

20. Reduce $\frac{144}{216}$ to lowest terms.

21. What is the quotient of $7\frac{2}{3} \div 2\frac{1}{2}$? Leave the answer as a reduced improper fraction.

22. What is the lowest common denominator of 2, $\frac{3}{8}, \frac{21}{24},$ and $\frac{5}{36}$?

23. Gabriele has three 1-gallon cans of the same paint. One gallon is $\frac{1}{3}$ full. The second gallon is $\frac{1}{5}$ full, and the third is $\frac{3}{8}$ full. How much paint is there in total, expressed as gallons?

24. Subtract $45\frac{3}{4}$ from $92\frac{5}{10}$.

25. Add $\frac{1}{7} + \frac{3}{5} + \frac{2}{10}$.

26. Emma gets $9 per hour for the first 40 hours worked per week and time and a half for hours over that. If she works 48 hours one week, what fractional part of her paycheck is overtime?

For questions 27–30, fill in the blank with the correct symbol: <, >, or =.

27. $\dfrac{3}{54}$ ——— $\dfrac{3}{56}$

28. $\dfrac{5}{4}$ ——— $1\dfrac{1}{2}$

29. $\dfrac{7}{4}$ ——— $\dfrac{13}{8}$

30. $\dfrac{3}{54}$ ——— $\dfrac{9}{162}$

Convert to improper fractions.

31. $1\dfrac{1}{4}$

32. $6\dfrac{7}{8}$

33. $12\dfrac{7}{10}$

Convert to mixed numbers, reducing fractions as needed.

34. $\dfrac{17}{4}$

35. $\dfrac{124}{11}$

36. $\dfrac{92}{72}$

For questions 37–41, write the letter shown on the number line that corresponds to the given number.

37. $3\dfrac{2}{3}$

38. $-1\dfrac{1}{2}$

39. $1\dfrac{1}{2}$

40. $6\dfrac{4}{5}$

41. $-\dfrac{3}{4}$

What number is presented by each of the following points on the number line?

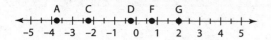

Calculate:

47. $64^{\frac{1}{3}}$

42. Point A:

48. $16^{-\frac{1}{2}}$

43. Point C:

49. $\left(-\dfrac{1}{3}\right)^2$

44. Point D:

50. $\left(\dfrac{2}{5}\right)^3$

45. Point F:

46. Point G:

CHAPTER 4

Decimal Numbers and Operations

Directions: Answer the following questions. For multiple-choice questions, choose the best answer. For other questions, write your answer in the space provided or the space below the question. Answers begin on page 92.

Use the symbols <, >, and = to state the correct relationship between the two numbers.

1. 10.008 _____ 10.0008

2. 0.10235 _____ 0.1235

3. 19.020 _____ 19.02

4. −11.954 _____ 11.945

5. 1.7×10^{-3} _____ -1.7×10^{3}

6. $(-6 \times 10^{6}) \times (-2 \times 10^{2}) =$
   A. -12×10^{8}
   B. 3×10^{4}
   C. 1.2×10^{9}
   D. -1.2×10^{9}

7. Which number below will give the sum of zero when added to 1.235?
   A. 1.235
   B. −1.235
   C. 2.470
   D. −2.470

8. Add 12.389 + 4.3950.

9. Add 34.56 + 13.23.

10. Multiply 7.454 × 2.3.

11. Divide 21.9555 ÷ 1.23.

12. Divide 1.80264 ÷ 0.203.

13. Multiply 45.55 × 15.

14. Tony fills his car with gas. His tank holds 14.0 gallons of gas. He pumps 8.37 gallons into the tank. If his car averages 27.6 miles per gallon, how far could he have driven before running out of gas had he not stopped to fill up? Give your answer to the nearest whole mile.

15. Juniata pays $132.50 a month in car payments and $675.00 for rent. She spends an average of $512.50 a month for utilities, food, and other necessities. She has savings of $3300. How many months of expenses does she have saved?

16. Terrance pays school taxes at the rate of 63.55 cents per $1000 dollars of assessed value of his family's home. His family home has an assessed value of $235,500. What is his school tax bill for the year, to the nearest penny?

17. The average distance from Earth to Mars is 2.25×10^8 kilometers. Radio waves travel at approximately 3.0×10^5 kilometers per second. On average, how many seconds does it take for a radio signal to go from Mars to Earth?

18. Subtract 52.7 – 16.23.

19. On the number line, what is the distance between –1.45 and –8.34?

20. On the number line, what is the distance between –1.989 and 2.735?

21. In the number 123.4556, the value of the underlined number is expressed in

    A. tenths.
    B. hundredths.
    C. thousandths.
    D. hundreds.

22. In which number below does the digit 5 represent the greatest value?

    A. 12.354
    B. 0.543
    C. 1.2354
    D. 15.2534

23. Illya bought 0.460 pounds of meat at $5.50 per pound. How much did the meat cost?

24. Svetlana bought 4 cans of soup for $1.35 each, a pound of hamburger for $3.29, and a loaf of bread for $2.10. There is no sales tax on food in her state. She gave the cashier a $20.00 bill. How much change should she receive?

25. Alan needs 7 quarters to do his laundry. What is the most he could spend from a $20.00 bill and still have enough left to wash his clothes?

26. One week Sam worked 32.75 hours at his job, which pays $17.50 per hour. How much did he earn that week before taxes and other deductions? Round to the nearest cent.

27. A seamstress receives $0.95 for every shirt sleeve she sews. If she sews an average of 15 sleeves an hour, how much will she make per hour?

28. If a rocket uses 150 kilograms of fuel to orbit 1 kilogram of matter, how many kilograms of fuel will be needed to orbit 6×10^4 kilograms of matter?

    A. 900×10^5 kilograms
    B. 2.5×10^6 kilograms
    C. 4.0×10^4 kilograms
    D. 9.0×10^6 kilograms

29. Sammie put 11.74 gallons of gasoline in her car at a cost of $3.459 per gallon. How much did she pay for the gasoline, rounded to the nearest cent?

30. If gasoline costs $4.599 a gallon, how many gallons can one buy for $20.00?

   A. 2.70 gallons
   B. 4.34 gallons
   C. 4.35 gallons
   D. 4.50 gallons

31. The cost of electricity in Sara's town is $0.265 per kilowatt hour. If she uses 1050 kilowatt hours of electricity in July, what will her electric bill be for that month?

32. The area of an oriental rug is calculated by multiplying its length by its width. What is the area of a rug that is 9.45 feet wide by 12.15 feet long? Round to two decimal places.

Use long division to convert the rational numbers below to their decimal equivalents.

33. $\frac{5}{8} =$

34. $\frac{3}{50} =$

35. $\frac{7}{64} =$

36. There are 6.02×10^{23} atoms in one cubic centimeter of a certain material. How many cubic centimeters does one atom take up? Express your answer in scientific notation and to two decimal places.

37. Al's commission for selling homes works out so he gets $0.0125 out of every dollar of the sales price. What is Al's commission on a $150,000 house?

38. Cal installs new tires and gets paid $1.17 per tire or gets paid $10.50 per hour for 8 hours, whichever is greater. How much more does he make on a day when he installs 85 tires than he would make if he received just his hourly wage?

39. Maribel pays $3.98 a yard for cloth. She buys 3.45 yards. How much does she pay? Round to the nearest cent.

40. It is roughly 93,000,000 miles from Earth to the sun. A scientist would express this number as

   A. 93,000,000 miles
   B. 93×10^6 miles
   C. 9.3×10^7 miles
   D. 0.0093×10^9 miles

41. The distance from Earth to the sun is 1 astronomical unit (AU) or 1.496×10^9 kilometers. If Mercury is 0.39 AU from the sun, how many kilometers from the sun is it?

   A. 10.79×10^6 kilometers
   B. 5.8×10^9 kilometers
   C. 1.079×10^7 kilometers
   D. 5.8×10^8 kilometers

42. Michelle has a $421.55 per month car payment. If she needs to pay a total of $19,500, including interest, how many months from now will she make her last payment?

43. An excellent 1-carat diamond sells for $1025. If one carat is 7.05×10^{-3} ounces, how much would an ounce of excellent diamonds cost, to the nearest dollar?

44. Subtract 100 − 52.72.

45. Peter has a job that pays $17.50 per hour for 40 hours per week, and he is paid each Friday. This week the company deducted $44.94 for Social Security, $10.50 for Medicare, $7.00 for State Disability Insurance, and $79.50 for Income Tax Withholding. What is Peter's take-home pay this week if he has no other deductions?

46. An irregular piece of property that Kerry wants to fence has sides that measure 12.35 meters, 123.56 meters, 111.23 meters, 73.4 meters, and 45.65 meters. How many meters of fencing will Kerry use, assuming a gap of 7.50 meters is needed for a gate?

47. The Earth's mass is 5.9742×10^{24} kilograms, while the moon's mass is 7.36×10^{22} kilograms. What is an estimate of the sum of the masses, expressed in scientific notation?

48. Write 6.022×10^{-5} in standard form.

49. Ken Johnson's place is located 17.35 km due west of the center of town on Route 17. Willy Hester's place is located 11.23 kilometers due west of the center of town, also on Route 17. How far from each other do the two neighbors live?

50. Donny lives 5.7 miles due west of the center of town on Route 45. His friend Sue lives 8.6 miles due east of the center of town, also on Route 45. Donny's car holds 13.5 gallons of gas and gets 32.5 miles a gallon. How many round trips can he make to see Sue without running out of gas?

CHAPTER 5
Ratios, Rates, and Proportions

Directions: Answer the following questions. For multiple-choice questions, choose the best answer. For other questions, write your answer in the space provided or the space below the question. Answers begin on page 94.

1. Which answer expresses the ratio *10 feet to 12 feet* as a fraction in lowest terms?

   A. $\frac{10}{12}$

   B. $\frac{12}{10}$

   C. $\frac{5}{6}$

   D. $\frac{6}{5}$

2. Write the ratio *21 students to 28 students* as a fraction in lowest terms.

3. Which answer expresses the rate *24 miles per 36 minutes* as a fraction in lowest terms?

   A. $\frac{24}{36}$

   B. $\frac{2}{3}$

   C. $\frac{3 \text{ minutes}}{2 \text{ miles}}$

   D. $\frac{2 \text{ miles}}{3 \text{ minutes}}$

4. Write the rate *20 leaves to 8 twigs* as a fraction in lowest terms.

5. Which answer expresses the rate *200 miles per 4 hours* as a unit rate?

   A. $\frac{200 \text{ miles}}{4 \text{ hours}}$

   B. $50\frac{\text{miles}}{\text{hours}}$

   C. $\frac{1 \text{ hour}}{50 \text{ miles}}$

   D. $\frac{4 \text{ hours}}{200 \text{ miles}}$

6. Write the rate *42 ounces per 5 mugs* as a unit rate. Write your answer as a decimal number.

7. In the first paragraph of an essay, Carmen wrote 70 words in 6 sentences. Which answer expresses this as a unit rate?

   A. $11\frac{2}{3}\frac{\text{words}}{\text{sentence}}$

   B. $\frac{35 \text{ words}}{3 \text{ sentences}}$

   C. $\frac{3 \text{ sentences}}{35 \text{ words}}$

   D. $11\frac{2}{3}\frac{\text{sentences}}{\text{word}}$

8. Bud earned $750 for a 40-hour week. What is Bud's rate of pay? Write your answer as a decimal.

9. Jakob built $\frac{3}{4}$ of a model in $\frac{1}{2}$ of a week. At what rate did Jakob build the model? Express your answer as a mixed number.

10. 2 packets of drink mix should be mixed with 3 quarts of water. Use the double number line to find how many packets of drink mix to mix with 54 quarts of water.

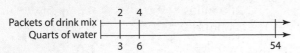

Packets of drink mix   2 4
Quarts of water   3 6   54

A. 30 packets
B. 33 packets
C. 36 packets
D. 39 packets

11. A hot dog vendor at a ballpark prepares for selling many hot dogs at the same time by preparing a table of costs per number of hot dogs. Help the vendor complete the table.

Hot dogs	1	2	3	4
Costs	1.50	3.00	4.50	6.00

Hot dogs	5	6	7	8	9
Costs					

12. Maria takes 7 minutes to clear a stack of 12 books for resale at the student bookstore. How long will it take her to clear a stack of 28 books?

A. $15\frac{2}{3}$ minutes

B. $16\frac{1}{3}$ minutes

C. $16\frac{2}{3}$ minutes

D. $17\frac{1}{3}$ minutes

13. Tinytown has all of its 132 citizens living on the 40 square miles within its town limits. What is the population density of Tinytown in persons per square mile?

A. 3.1 persons per square mile
B. 3.2 persons per square mile
C. 3.3 persons per square mile
D. 3.4 persons per square mile

14. Marty, a letter carrier, has noticed that the time it takes him to complete his route is proportional to the weight of his mailbag when he leaves the post office. If it takes him 3 hours to deliver 8 pounds of mail, how long does it take him to deliver 10 pounds of mail?

A. $3\frac{1}{4}$ hours

B. $3\frac{1}{3}$ hours

C. $3\frac{2}{3}$ hours

D. $3\frac{3}{4}$ hours

15. Johnny Jalopy drove 240 miles from Dallas to Houston in 3.5 hours. What was his rate of speed? Express your answer to the nearest mile per hour.

16. 127 millimeters is exactly 5 inches. How many millimeters is 8 inches?

A. 203 millimeters
B. 203.2 millimeters
C. 2.6 millimeters
D. 206.4 millimeters

17. A piece of wood has a mass of 20 grams and a volume of 25 cm^3. What is the density of the wood in grams per cm^3?

A. 0.8 g/cm^3
B. 0.9 g/cm^3
C. 1.2 g/cm^3
D. 1.3 g/cm^3

18. Celia bought 24 bottles of orange juice for her daughter's birthday party for a total price of $30. What was the unit price of each bottle of orange juice?

19. Jack drew $\frac{5}{8}$ of a picture in $\frac{5}{12}$ of an hour.

    What is Jack's picture-drawing rate in pictures/hour?

    A. $\frac{2}{3}$ picture/hour

    B. $\frac{3}{4}$ picture/hour

    C. $1\frac{1}{2}$ pictures/hour

    D. $1\frac{3}{4}$ pictures/hour

20. The scale on a map of Ohio says that on the map, 2 inches equals 35 miles. What is the distance between Cleveland and Cincinnati, which are 14 inches apart on the map?

    A. 140 miles
    B. 175 miles
    C. 210 miles
    D. 245 miles

21. On the plans for a building, the drawing of a wall measures $3\frac{1}{3}$ inches tall by $9\frac{1}{2}$ inches wide. The scale says that 1 inch equals 6 feet. What will be the dimensions of the wall once it is built?

    A. 19 feet tall by 55 feet wide
    B. 19 feet tall by 57 feet wide
    C. 20 feet tall by 55 feet wide
    D. 20 feet tall by 57 feet wide

22. A large-screen television has an aspect ratio of 16:9. How tall is the screen if it is 96 centimeters wide?

    A. 48 centimeters
    B. 54 centimeters
    C. 56 centimeters
    D. 60 centimeters

23. Dosage information for a drug specifies that 2.5 milliliters should be administered for every 20 kilograms of a patient's mass. How much of the drug should be given to a patient whose mass is 90 kilograms?

    A. 11.25 milliliters
    B. 11.5 milliliters
    C. 11.75 milliliters
    D. 12 milliliters

24. A recipe that serves 4 people calls for $3\frac{1}{2}$ cups of flour. Suzy plans to serve this dish to 10 friends and relatives at Thanksgiving. How much flour does she need?

    A. 8 cups

    B. $8\frac{1}{4}$ cups

    C. $8\frac{1}{2}$ cups

    D. $8\frac{3}{4}$ cups

25. Henri put 12.4 gallons of gas in his car to fill it up. Having reset his trip odometer on his previous visit to the gas station, during which he filled up the tank, he noticed that he has driven 298.9 miles. What is his mileage?

    A. 23.9 miles per gallon
    B. 24.1 miles per gallon
    C. 24.3 miles per gallon
    D. 24.5 miles per gallon

26. A plastic model company sells a model of a battleship at a $\frac{1}{288}$ scale. The battleship is 864 feet long. How long is the model?

    A. 2 feet
    B. 2.5 feet
    C. 3 feet
    D. 3.5 feet

27. Fran drives 27 miles on her paper route in 45 minutes. It takes her 2 hours to drive the entire route at the same rate. How long is Fran's paper route?

    A. 72 miles
    B. 74 miles
    C. 76 miles
    D. 78 miles

28. A scale drawing with a scale of 1 inch = 3 feet is redrawn so that 1 inch = 5 feet. What is the new length of the side of a square that was 2 inches on the old drawing?

    A. 0.8 inch
    B. 0.9 inch
    C. 1.1 inches
    D. 1.2 inches

29. A photo that measures 2 inches wide by 3 inches tall is blown up so that it is 8 inches wide. How tall is the new photo?

    A. 11 inches
    B. 12 inches
    C. 13 inches
    D. 14 inches

30. A parade starts in a stadium with a lap around a football field, then continues through the city for an additional 3 miles. If a marching band takes 12 minutes to march the $\frac{1}{4}$ - mile track around the field, how long will it take to march the entire route, at the same rate?

    A. 2 hours 12 minutes
    B. 2 hours 24 minutes
    C. 2 hours 36 minutes
    D. 2 hours 48 minutes

31. Julio walks 264 feet per minute. What is his rate in miles per hour? (Hint: 1 mile = 5280 feet.)

    A. 3 miles per hour
    B. 3.5 miles per hour
    C. 4 miles per hour
    D. 4.5 miles per hour

32. A box of a dozen granola bars costs $3.60. What is the unit cost?

    A. $0.27 per bar
    B. $0.30 per bar
    C. $0.32 per bar
    D. $0.33 per bar

33. Brad burns 4.5 gallons of gas driving 99 miles. How far can he drive with a full tank of 16 gallons?

    A. 340 miles
    B. 348 miles
    C. 352 miles
    D. 360 miles

34. Are the ratios 14:21 and 48:72 in proportion?

    Check _____ Yes or _____ No.

35. Gasoline costs $3.15 per gallon. Which equation shows the total cost C of buying g gallons of gasoline?

    A. $C = \frac{g}{3.15}$
    B. $g = 3.15C$
    C. $g = \frac{3.15}{C}$
    D. $C = 3.15g$

36. What is the unit rate in the table?

Crates	1	2	3	4	5	6	7	8	9
Pounds	40	80	120	160	200	240	280	320	360

    A. 40 crates per pound
    B. 40 pounds per crate

    C. $\frac{1}{40}$ pounds per crate

    D. $\frac{1}{80}$ crates per pound

37. Marvin's pay is modeled by the equation $P = 13.25t$. What is the unit rate in the equation?

38. Fill in the empty cells in the tables to determine which ratio is smaller, $\frac{3}{5}$ or $\frac{5}{8}$.

Number	3	
Price	5	40

Number	5	
Price	8	40

39. Dennis drove 300 miles in 5 hours. Write an equation, using Dennis' unit rate, that expresses the relationship between the time t he drives and the distance D he covers.

    A. $t = \dfrac{60}{D}$

    B. $D = \dfrac{60}{t}$

    C. $t = 60D$
    D. $D = 60t$

40. Are the ratios 18:81 and 34:154 in proportion?

41. Jimmy earned $48.75 washing cars for 5 hours. Johnny earned $58.32 mowing lawn for 6 hours. Who had the higher rate of pay?

42. A bookstore is having a sale, offering a discount on all books in the store. A book with a regular price of $12.95 is on sale for $7.77. At the same discount rate, what is the selling price of a book with a regular price of $18.50?

43. Last year, the manager of a baseball team bought the season's supply of 60 baseballs from a sporting goods store for $1620. This year he is buying baseballs from the same store at the same price, but he hasn't decided how many to buy. Write an equation giving the total price T of n baseballs.

44. A city is planning to place a 22-foot-high statue in a local park. The artist who earned the commission is working from a model that is 18 inches high. A feature on the model measure 3 inches across. How large will the feature on the completed statue be?

45. How far does a car travel in 1 minute at the rate of 75 miles per hour?

46. The chef at a restaurant gets 20 bowls of soup from a 5-quart pot. How much more soup could he get from a 9-quart pot?

47. According to the 2010 U.S. Census, San Francisco has a population of 805,000 living in a land area of 47 square miles, while Poplar Hills, Kentucky, has 362 citizens occupying 0.02 square miles of land. Which has the higher population density?

48. Jeanine keeps careful records on the performance of her automobile. The table shows the amount of fuel she recorded for trips of different lengths:

Distance (miles)	72	144	192	288	336	360
Fuel (gallons)	3	6	8	12	14	15

Write an equation relating the trip distance (D) to the amount of fuel used (f). What does the multiplier represent?

49. The speed of light is roughly 186,000 miles per second. How many minutes does it take for light to arrive from the sun, which is 93,000,000 miles away?

50. Bulk flour costs $1.79 per pound. How many pounds of flour can be purchased for $17.37?

CHAPTER 6

Percents and Applications

Directions: Answer the following questions. For multiple-choice questions, choose the best answer. For other questions, write your answer in the space next to or below the question. Answers begin on page 97.

Express each decimal number as a percent.

1. 0.175

2. 0.8

3. 6.605

4. 15.20

5. 0.0017

Express each fraction or mixed number as a percent rounded to the nearest hundredth.

6. $\frac{6}{10}$

7. $\frac{2}{3}$

8. $\frac{7}{5}$

9. 3

10. $2\frac{7}{8}$

Express each percent as a fraction or mixed number reduced to lowest terms.

11. 32.5%

12. 60%

13. 6%

14. 185%

15. 0.35%

Express each percent as a decimal number.

16. 11%

17. 4%

18. 2756%

19. $7\frac{3}{16}$%

20. 0.0076%

21. A pair of gloves retails for $17.89. If the sales tax is $8\frac{1}{2}$%, what is the total cost of the gloves?

22. A game console that lists for $159.95 is on sale at a discount of 15%. If there is a $5\frac{1}{4}$% sales tax, how much will Jane pay for the console? (Round up to a whole cent.)

23. A bag of Spot's dog food usually costs $36.99. It is on sale today at 20% off. In addition, his owner has a coupon good for 10% off any purchase. What is the cost of the dog food before sales tax?

24. Susan unloaded 168 boxes of books from a shipment of 1052. What percentage of the shipment is left to unload? (Round to a whole number.)

25. Rufus owes $9250 in no-interest student loans. After paying off 32% of what he owes, how much will he still have to pay?

    A. $6290
    B. $2960
    C. $7215
    D. $3046

26. Imelda bought a guitar with no money down and has a loan for $1150 at 6% per year. If she pays off the loan after 4 months, what is the total cost of the guitar?

27. Sydney buys her textbooks online and spends $1147. The sales tax in her town is $5\frac{3}{4}$%, but the bookseller does not charge tax on Internet sales. Before she pays for shipping, how much has she saved by not paying sales tax? (Round to the nearest cent.)

28. Ashanti's Bike Store makes a profit of 17.5% on sales. If this month's profit is $2175, how much did the store sell this month? (Round to the nearest cent.)

29. After paying a $6\frac{1}{4}$% sales tax, Jerome paid $135.20 for a set of Blu-ray discs that listed for $149.70 but was on sale at a discount. To the nearest whole percent, what was the discount on the set before sales tax?

30. To be considered a periodical under the post office's rules, a magazine must have no more than 25% advertising content. The present issue of the magazine that Aram manages has 172 pages but is 28.5% ads. How many pages must Aram convert from ads to non-advertising content to meet the post office's requirement?

31. There are about 150 million registered voters in the United States. Pollsters question 2056 of them to get an accurate prediction of an upcoming vote, to a plus or minus 4% accuracy. Approximately what percent of the voters is this?

    A. 0.0014%
    B. 0.014%
    C. 0.14%
    D. 1.4%

32. Bill's Bikes has sold $3036.00 worth of merchandise this month. That is a 15% increase over last month. And last month saw a 10% increase over the month before. How much merchandise did Bill's Bikes sell two months ago?

33. There are 207,634,000 Americans who are eligible to vote, but only 150 million are registered to vote. In the 2012 presidential election, only 57% of registered voters participated. What percentage of eligible voters does this represent?

34. Salome is looking at a watch that costs $9.99, and she has $10.00 to spend. But sales tax is 6%. How much of a discount, expressed as a percentage, must the store offer for Salome to be able to buy it?

35. The number of traffic accidents in our city has dropped by 17% this year. If last year's total was 475, what is this year's total?

    A. 281
    B. 394
    C. 400
    D. 600

36. A fully fueled AeroTrans 474 passenger jet airplane weighs 987,000 pounds at takeoff. It carries 422,000 pounds of fuel. What percent of the aircraft's takeoff weight is fuel?

37. Levi paid $180.00 for a set of dishes listed at $225.00. What was the discount, to the nearest percent?

38. For telephone and Internet service, Jerry pays $63.70 a month, including 7.95% in various taxes. What is the cost of the telephone and Internet service before tax?

    A. $68.76
    B. $61.95
    C. $59.00
    D. $35.48

39. If Leda pays her bill for duck food early, she can get a 1.5% discount. How much can she save on a bill of $3720?

40. Tonya gets a 15% discount on merchandise she buys at work. If she pays $170 for some merchandise, what would it have cost her without the discount?

    A. $113.30
    B. $165.00
    C. $200.00
    D. $225.45

41. Tom buys an investment. Its value drops by 50% one month. The next month, though, its value increases by 50%. What is the result at the end of the second month?

    A. The value has not changed.
    B. The value has increased by 50%.
    C. The value has decreased by 25%.
    D. The value has decreased by 50%.

42. Federal tax on airline tickets is 7.5%. How much does a ticket for a round trip to Orlando from Chicago, listed at $269, cost after taxes?

    A. $289.18
    B. $299.22
    C. $314.29
    D. $370.75

43. Last year 1,320,000 people visited the state fair. This year 1,544,400 visited. What percentage increase or decrease was this, to the nearest whole percent?

44. Yaakov paid one month's interest of $76.00 on a $5000 loan. What was the interest rate on the loan, expressed as a percentage, per year?

    A. 1.52%
    B. 15.2%
    C. 1.82%
    D. 18.2%

45. Elita bought a scarf on sale for $14.49 after a 16% discount. What was the scarf's original price?

    A. $17.25
    B. $17.34
    C. $12.88
    D. $14.95

46. Sal made an investment that performed as shown in the chart below. What was the net gain or loss of the investment at the end of four months?

Month	Percent change from prior month
1	+10%
2	−5%
3	+2%
4	−7%

47. Salem pays 6.2% Social Security tax, 1.45% Medicare, and 14% federal income tax withholding each pay period. How much is left after taxes from a paycheck of $718.15?

48. Joe, a plumber, buys a part on sale at 25% off. In addition, he gets 15% off his entire order. If the part's list price is $555.00, what is its cost after the discounts?

    A. $194.25
    B. $208.13
    C. $333.00
    D. $353.81

49. Tara makes a batch of tortilla dough with 100 pounds flour, 9 pounds of shortening, and 3 pounds of baking soda. What percent of the batch is shortening?

    A. 8%
    B. 9%
    C. 3%
    D. 12%

50. Ishmael sells yachts and sold $90,000 worth of yachts this month. That is an increase of 20% over last month's sales. But last month was 20% less than the month before. What were Ishmael's sales two months ago?

CHAPTER 7
Probability and Statistics

Directions: Answer the following questions. For multiple-choice questions, choose the best answer. For other questions, write your answer in the space below the question. Answers begin on page 99.

For questions 1–4, use this table of experimental data.

X	2	7	4	5	9	1	6	3	11	8
Y	14	47	29	35	63	8	42	22	77	56

1. What kind of probability model can be made from these data if X is the input and Y the result?

   A. None, the data are random.
   B. one in which the data are approximately proportional
   C. one in which the data are inversely proportional
   D. one in which the data are related by a power of 2

2. Which equation below expresses the model?

   A. There is no equation possible.
   B. $Y = 7X + a$
   C. $Y = X^2 + a$
   D. $Y = 7X$

3. What is the most probable reason that not all the data fit the model exactly?

   A. The data are poorly recorded.
   B. There is no relation between the data and the model.
   C. Each data point is subject to random effects.
   D. There is no reason.

4. If the best-fit curve on the scatter plot of these data is a straight line passing through the origin, what CANNOT be said about the relationship between variables?

   A. The two variables are proportional.
   B. The equation relating the variables will need an added constant.
   C. The data are probably not random.
   D. The slope of the best-fit line approximates the proportion between variables.

For questions 5–8, use the data set {1, 3, 14, 28, 2, 18, 27, 86, 34, 45, 44, 36, 21, 11, 51, 23, 37, 52, 29, 41, 33, 19, 24, 38, 15, 87}.

5. What is the median of the data set?

6. Draw a histogram of the data set, grouping the data by multiples of 10, for example, 1–10, 11–20, 21–30, and so on.

7. Which, if any, of the data might be considered outliers?

8. Is the median a good measure of the center?

   Check _____ Yes or _____ No.

9. Given a large sample of families with three children, what percent of the families will have all boys?

10. In a family with three children, what is the percentage probability of all the children being the same gender?

11. In a large sample of families with three children, in what percentage of those families would you expect to have at least one girl?

12. Construct a probability tree for the different arrangements of genders of children in a family with three children. Use this tree to determine the probability of a family having two girls and one boy.

13. Write the proper word in each blank.

    heads   mean   mode   median
    random   result   tails   three

    Given a fair coin, the most likely _____

    of six separate flips is _____

    _____ and _____ _____,

    which is also the _____ and the

    _____ of the_____ data set.

For questions 14–17, use the data set {2, 11, 8, 10, 6, 11, 7, 14, 20, 9, 1}.

14. What is the mean of the data set?

    A. 1
    B. 7
    C. 9
    D. 11

15. What is the median value of this data set?

    A. 1
    B. 7
    C. 9
    D. 19

16. What is the mode of this data set?

    A. 7
    B. 8
    C. 9
    D. 11

17. What is the range?

    A. 3
    B. 6
    C. 15
    D. 19

18. Said is getting dressed without turning on the light so he won't wake his brother. He is picking socks, but cannot tell the colors of the socks in his sock drawer. He knows that there are 12 black socks, 8 red socks, and 16 brown socks in the drawer. He picks out a sock and sees that it is brown. What is the probability that he will need to make at least three picks to get a pair?

19. Said has now drawn a brown sock and a black sock. What is the probability that he will make a matched pair on his next pick?

20. Said now has picked 1 brown, 1 red, and 1 black sock. What is the probability that he will NOT make a matched pair with his next pick?

    A. 100%
    B. 67%
    C. 33%
    D. 0%

Use the following for questions 21–23.

Angela worked at a department store checking the sales made by various salespersons. She developed this chart.

Sales	# Salespersons
$0–$50	1
$51–$100	3
$101–$150	7
$151–$200	6
$201–$250	4

21. If a salesperson is picked at random, what is the probability that a person who sold between $201 and $250 worth of merchandise will be chosen?

22. Using the same data above, what is the probability that a salesperson picked at random will have sold more than $150 worth of merchandise?

23. What is the modal class of this week's sales?

    A. 0–$50
    B. $51–$100
    C. $101–$150
    D. $151–$200

The partial result of a survey of factory staff is given below.

Staff	Male	Female	Total
Assembler	7	3	10
Finisher	2	11	13

24. What is the probability that an employee picked at random will be a female or a finisher?

25. Given a fair coin, what is the probability of throwing four heads in four throws?

26. Given a fair coin, what is the probability of throwing heads, tails, heads in that order for three throws?

27. Jerry is blindfolded and picking from pieces of paper with consecutive numbers from 1 to 30 written on them, to set up softball teams. If he has already selected the numbers 10, 5, and 21 without returning them to the pool, what is the probability that his next pick will be the number 1?

Use the following for questions 28–30.

A tree diagram for drilling wildcat wells is given below. The numbers are decimal probabilities.

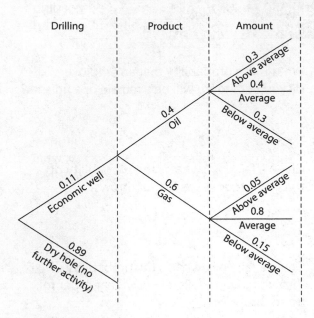

28. The most likely occurrence of a productive well is

   A. an average oil well.
   B. an average gas well.
   C. an above-average gas well.
   D. an above-average oil well.

29. The least likely productive well is

   A. an average oil well.
   B. an average gas well.
   C. an above-average gas well.
   D. an above-average oil well.

30. Assume a profitable economic well produces an average income of $23 million, while the average cost of a dry hole is $1.2 million. How much profit can be expected from a 100-well drilling program?

31. A fair coin is tossed six times. What is the probability that at least one head will be tossed?

32. Julie flips a coin four times and gets four tails. What can she conclude from this experiment?

   A. The coin is not fair.
   B. If the next throw is heads, then the coin is fair.
   C. If the next throw is tails, the coin is not fair.
   D. Nothing conclusive about the fairness of the coin can be said.

33. Tommy is a soccer coach and is trying to decide how to play three halfbacks. He has three players to fill left halfback, center halfback, and right halfback positions. How many distinct arrangements could he make with three players?

34. The coach in the last problem now has six players to choose from to fill the three positions. How many different arrangements of three does he have to choose from?

35. A teacher has 10 test questions to choose from to make up a 5-question section of an exam. How many combinations of questions are available?

36. The mathematics department at a small college has six women and eight men as instructors. The dean must select a committee of two women and two men for peer review duties. How many different possible committees are there?

37. If the committee above were selected at random, what is the probability that the first pick would be a woman?

38. If the committee were selected at random without regard to the requirement that it be gender-balanced, what is the probability, as a percentage, that it would end up all women?

39. An American roulette wheel has 38 numbers. Two are colored green; the other 36 are equally divided between red and black. You may play red or black. If your color comes up, you win, but if a green number comes up, no one wins. What is the percentage probability you will win if you bet on red?

40. What is the probability that six letters selected from the alphabet will be picked in alphabetical order?

41. Out of 100 people surveyed, 52 owned cats, 44 owned dogs, and 4 owned guinea pigs. Portray these data in a pie chart.

42. In a famous mathematical problem, a salesman must fly to several cities without visiting the same one twice. The problem is to find the most economical itinerary, but to do this a computer must calculate each possible itinerary. If there are seven cities to be visited, how many itineraries must the computer calculate?

43. In a group of 30 people, 6 are from California. If 3 people are selected from the group, what is the probability that at least 1 will be from somewhere other than California?

44. An automobile manufacturer offers a choice of five colors, three engine sizes, and two transmissions. How many unique cars can be made from these choices?

45. One hundred tickets are sold for a raffle. You bought five tickets and won neither the first nor second prize. What is the probability of your winning third prize?

46. A combination lock has numbers from 0 to 30 and takes a three-number combination to open it. If you walk up and try all the combinations that have three identical numbers, like 12-12-12 or 7-7-7, what is the probability you will open the lock?

47. A statistician tosses a thumbtack in the air 250 times. He records that the thumbtack lands point-up 165 times. What is the probability that the thumbtack will land point-up on a single toss?

48. Sylvia has credit hours and grades as shown on the chart. Her school gives 4 points for an A, 3 points for a B, 2 points for a C, 1 point for a D, and nothing for an F. What is her grade point average, the weighted mean of her grades?

Grades	A	B	C	D	F
Credit hours	16	27	18	8	1
Grade points	4	3	2	1	0

49. Terri has grades of 75, 87, 96, 76, and 88. What is the lowest grade she may get on the final exam, which carries a double weight, to get a grade of B? (B ranges between 80 and 89 points.)

A. 80

B. 69

C. 58

D. It is impossible for her to not get a B with those grades.

50. What grade does Terri need to get an A in the course if an A requires an average of 90?

A. 90

B. 95

C. 100

D. It is impossible for her to get an A with those grades.

CHAPTER 8

Geometry

Directions: Answer the following questions. For multiple-choice questions, choose the best answer. For other questions, write your answer in the space below the question. Answers begin on page 103.

1. Sam has a garden broken into three plots as shown below. The areas of two of the plots are given in square feet and the length of one side of each of two plots is given. What is the total area of the garden in square feet?

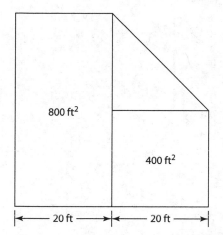

800 ft²

400 ft²

|← 20 ft →|← 20 ft →|

2. If Sam wants to replace the perimeter fence, how many feet of fencing, which is sold in whole feet, will he need to buy?

   A. 149 feet
   B. 148 feet
   C. 120 feet
   D. 50 feet

3. What happens to the length c of the hypotenuse of a right triangle if the lengths a and b of the two legs are doubled?

4. What happens to the area of a right triangle if each side is doubled in length?

   A. It increases by a factor of 1.41.
   B. It decreases by a factor of 1.41.
   C. It increases by a factor of 4.
   D. It decreases by a factor of 4.

5. Andrea must paint an antique sign composed of three spheres, each of which has a diameter of 12 inches. Each can of paint covers 288 square inches. How many cans of paint must Andrea buy to do the job?

6. Given a square 4 feet on a side, what is the area of the largest circle that fits within the square?

   A. 25.14 square feet
   B. 12.56 square feet
   C. 6.28 square feet
   D. 14 square feet

7. For the square in the problem above, what is the area outside the circle but inside the square?

8. A rectangle 6 feet wide has a circle of diameter 6 feet inscribed within. How high is the rectangle if the areas within the circle and outside the circle are equal?

   A. 3.42 feet
   B. 6.28 feet
   C. 7.74 feet
   D. 9.42 feet

9. Kathryn is designing a hood for a barbecue grill. The top is to be 36 inches wide and has ends as shown in the illustration. How many square inches of sheet metal will be needed for the hood?

   A. 2100.6 square inches
   B. 2305.5 square inches
   C. 2919.6 square inches
   D. 3060.2 square inches

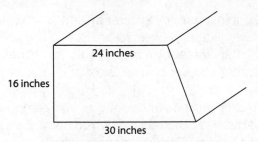

24 inches

16 inches

30 inches

10–19. Write the correct letter in the blanks to match the formula for surface area and volume on each figure.

   A. $\pi rl + \pi r^2$
   B. $4\pi r^2$
   C. $\pi r^2 h$
   D. $\frac{4}{3}\pi r^3$
   E. $bh + Pl$, where P is the perimeter of the base
   F. $\frac{1}{3}\pi r^2 h$
   G. $2hl + 2hw + 2lw$
   H. $2\pi r^2 + 2\pi rh$
   I. $\frac{1}{2}bhl$
   J. lwh

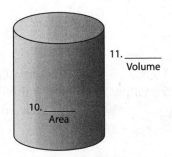

11. _____
    Volume

10. _____
    Area

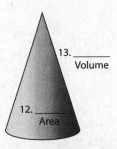

13. _____
    Volume

12. _____
    Area

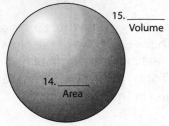

15. _____
    Volume

14. _____
    Area

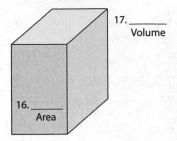

17. _____
    Volume

16. _____
    Area

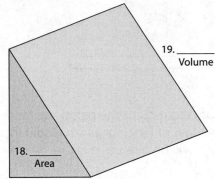

19. _____
    Volume

18. _____
    Area

20. What is the difference between the amount of water that can be held by a sphere of diameter 1 centimeter and a cube 1 centimeter on a side?

21. Triana has taken a job refinishing a large ice cream cone that hangs outside the Soda Spot. The sign is made of a half sphere of radius 1 foot atop a pointed cone with a top that has the same radius and that is 6 feet high. How many square feet of surface does Triana need to cover with new paint?

   A. 12.56 square feet
   B. 19.1 square feet
   C. 25.4 square feet
   D. 32.6 square feet

22. What is the perimeter of a right triangle whose height is twice its base and whose area is 72.25 square inches?

23. The area A of any regular polygon is equal to $A = \frac{1}{2}aP$, where a is the apothem (the distance from the center of the polygon measured perpendicular to a side) and P the perimeter. Given a regular hexagon inscribed in a circle with a radius of 6 centimeters, what is its area in square centimeters?

    A. 23.4 square centimeters
    B. 18.2 square centimeters
    C. 9.2 square centimeters
    D. 2.6 square centimeters

24. What is the area of a pentagon with a perimeter of 30 centimeters and an apothem of 4.13 centimeters?

25. Sandra has a trough that will hold water for her cattle. It is 11 feet long, and each end is a trapezoid with a bottom measure of 4 feet and a top measure of 6 feet. If the trough is 2 feet deep, how many cubic feet of water will it hold? The area of a trapezoid is found using $\frac{b_1 + b_2}{2} h$, where b_1 and b_2 are the lengths of the two bases and h is the height.

    A. 55 cubic feet
    B. 110 cubic feet
    C. 220 cubic feet
    D. 20 cubic feet

26. Adriana wishes to sell her special cactus apple preserves in cans holding 296 cubic centimeters each. Her canning machine works only with cans 7.5 centimeters in diameter. She needs to know how tall the cans will be so she can get labels printed. How tall will the cans be?

27. Assuming the labels must be 1 centimeter extra long to overlap and will be as tall as the can, what is the area of paper used for each label?

    A. 24.6 square centimeters
    B. 164.5 square centimeters
    C. 157.3 square centimeters
    D. 179.0 square centimeters

28. XYZ Paper Products is designing a package for a toy that will be shipped from an overseas factory to the United States. The packages are 6 inches wide, 12 inches long, and 3 inches high. A standard cardboard box is 24 × 24 × 24 inches and holds 13,824 cubic inches. How many packages will fit in one standard cardboard box?

29. If each package above is made of polystyrene $\frac{1}{16}$ inch thick, how many cubic inches of polystyrene will go into making each package?

30. A regulation soccer ball has a circumference of 68 centimeters, and a regulation basketball has a circumference of 75.5 centimeters. What is the difference in their volumes?

    A. 1900 cubic centimeters
    B. 1958 cubic centimeters
    C. 2060 cubic centimeters
    D. 2152 cubic centimeters

31. Given a rectangular field 125 by 100 feet, what would be the length of the side of an equilateral triangle with the same perimeter?

32. What is the difference in the areas of the two fields?

33. Farmer Noir has a square plot measuring 660 feet on a side, which he wants to irrigate. Long ago, he used fences to divide the plot into four equal-sized square fields. He has two choices. He can tear down the fences and use one long pivot arm sprinkler that will irrigate a large circle centered at the middle of the plot. Otherwise, he can leave the fences up and irrigate each field separately with smaller pivot sprinklers. What is the difference in irrigated area between the two options?

   A. 2073 square feet
   B. 4147 square feet
   C. 8530 square feet
   D. 0 square feet

34. The company Con Tiki and Son is carpeting a recital hall at the local college. The hall is a square 125 feet on a side, with a semicircular performance area as shown in the illustration. How many square feet of carpeting are needed to do the job?

35. How long is the hypotenuse of a right triangle 24 square inches in area and with one leg 6 inches long?

36. Ahmed is creating a large balloon in the shape of a medical capsule for a drug company's Employee Day festivities. The balloon is a cylinder 50 feet long and 12 feet in diameter, capped at each end by half spheres 12 feet in diameter. How many cubic feet of gas is needed to fill the balloon?

   A. 6557 cubic feet
   B. 9623 cubic feet
   C. 13,137 cubic feet
   D. 22,405 cubic feet

37. Not including overlap for seams, how many square feet of cloth will Ahmed need for the pill-shaped balloon?

   A. 2336 square feet
   B. 1572 square feet
   C. 1385 square feet
   D. 1225 square feet

38. If the volume of a sphere is doubled, what happens to the radius?

   A. It increases by a factor of 2.
   B. It increases by a factor of 1.414.
   C. It increases by a factor of 1.26.
   D. It increases by a factor of 2.24.

39. Cal wants to run a zip line from the top of an 85-foot pole and have it reach a point 250 feet away, where the rider lets go 5 feet above a pool of water. What is the length of the wire?

40. The volume of a pyramid or a cone is $\frac{1}{3}Bh$, where B is the area of the base and h is the height. What is the height of a cone with the same volume as a pyramid with a square base 6 feet on a side and with a height of 20 feet?

   A. 225 feet
   B. 166.67 feet
   C. 196.3 feet
   D. 25.5 feet

41. Tina makes an hourglass that is 3 inches across the base and 12 inches high. If she fills the upper part of the hourglass to half its volume, how many cubic inches of sand will she need? (Her hourglass is two cones together, tip to tip.)

42. A cardboard box measures 12 inches high, 7 inches wide, and 9 inches deep. If another box measuring $3\frac{1}{2}$ by $4\frac{1}{2}$ inches is to have the same surface area, what will the box's third dimension need to be?

    A. $15\frac{3}{4}$ inches

    B. $18\frac{1}{4}$ inches

    C. $29\frac{29}{32}$ inches

    D. $30\frac{3}{15}$ inches

43. A formal garden as shown in the illustration is a square 50 feet on a side, with four half circles attached, one to each side. What is the total area of the garden?

44. What is the perimeter of the garden in the problem above?

45. What is the length of one edge of a cube that has a volume of 2,985,984 cubic inches?

46. A prism has ends that are right triangles. The length of one leg of the triangles is 7 units, and the hypotenuse is 11.4 units long. The prism has a volume of 787.5 cubic units. How high is the prism?

    A. 1.6 units
    B. 25 units
    C. 31.5 units
    D. 69.1 units

47. The box that a new printer cartridge comes in is 7 centimeters high. The ends are trapezoids with bases 11 centimeters and $7\frac{1}{2}$ centimeters and height $3\frac{1}{2}$ centimeters. What is the volume of the box?

    A. $26\frac{1}{4}$ cubic centimeters

    B. $32\frac{3}{8}$ cubic centimeters

    C. $111\frac{3}{4}$ cubic centimeters

    D. $226\frac{5}{8}$ cubic centimeters

    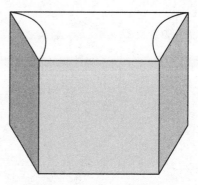

48. The area of an equilateral triangle of side length s is given by the formula $A = \frac{\sqrt{3}}{4}s^2$. What is the area of an equilateral triangle 15 feet on a side?

49. The area of an equilateral triangle of side length s is given by the formula $A = \frac{\sqrt{3}}{4}s^2$. An equilateral triangle has an area of 86.6 square feet. What is the length of one side?

    A. 14 feet
    B. 11.5 feet
    C. 7.0 feet
    D. 3.14 feet

50. A new design for a space station is being evaluated. A cross-section of the station is a regular hexagon with perimeter 360 feet, and the entire station is 500 feet long. What is the volume of the station?

CHAPTER 9

Polynomial and Rational Expressions

Directions: Answer the following questions. For multiple-choice questions, choose the best answer. For other questions, write your answer in the space below the question. Answers begin on page 107.

1. Combine like terms: $(2a + 5b - 7) + (a - 9b - 6)$.

    A. $2a - 4b - 13$
    B. $2a - 4b + 13$
    C. $3a - 4b - 13$
    D. $3a - 4b + 13$

2. Write $5(3x - 2y + 4)$ in an equivalent form without parentheses.

    A. $15x - 2y + 4$
    B. $15x - 10y + 20$
    C. $53x - 2y + 4$
    D. $53x - 52y + 54$

3. Subtract $(2x + 5) - (5x - 7)$.

    A. $-3x + 12$
    B. $3x - 2$
    C. $-3x - 2$
    D. $3x + 12$

4. Write "five more than twice a number" as an algebraic expression using the variable x.

5. Which of the following best describes the expression $7(y - 1)$?

    A. sum
    B. difference
    C. product
    D. quotient

6. Write "eight less than the cube of a number" as an algebraic expression using the variable x.

7. Evaluate $\frac{9}{5}C + 32$ for $C = -40$.

8. Which of the following best describes the expression $6x + 9y$?

    A. sum
    B. difference
    C. product
    D. quotient

9. In the expression $4x^2 + 6$, which quantity is a coefficient?

    A. 4
    B. x
    C. 2
    D. 6

10. Working for the census, Sam interviews seven fewer households than Sharon, who interviews twice as many households as Steve. If Steve interviews s households, how many households does Sam interview?

    A. $2s - 7s$
    B. $2(s - 7)$
    C. $2 - 7s$
    D. $2s - 7$

11. Add $(3x^2 + x - 2) + (x^2 - 4x + 7)$.

    A. $3x^2 - 4x + 5$
    B. $4x^2 - 3x + 5$
    C. $4x^4 - 3x^2 + 5$
    D. $3x^4 - 4x^2 + 5$

12. Subtract $(3x + 2y) - (2x + 3y)$.

    A. $x - y$
    B. $5x - y$
    C. $x - 5y$
    D. $5x - 5y$

13. Subtract $(6x^2 + 2x - 4) - (2x^2 - 5x + 1)$.

    A. $4x^2 - 3x - 3$
    B. $4x^2 - 3x - 5$
    C. $4x^2 + 7x - 5$
    D. $4x^2 + 7x - 3$

14. Use the properties of exponents to rewrite $x^3 \cdot x^6 \cdot x^2$.

    A. x^{11}
    B. x^{36}
    C. $3x^{11}$
    D. $3x^{36}$

15. Multiply $2x^4 \cdot 4x^5$.

    A. $6x^9$
    B. $8x^9$
    C. $6x^{20}$
    D. $8x^{20}$

16. Simplify $\dfrac{x^8}{x^2}$.

    A. $\dfrac{8}{2}$
    B. 4
    C. x^4
    D. x^6

17. Simplify $\dfrac{25x^9y^4}{15x^6y^{12}}$.

    A. $\dfrac{10x^3y}{x^2y^3}$
    B. $\dfrac{10x^3}{y^8}$
    C. $\dfrac{5x^3y}{3x^2y^3}$
    D. $\dfrac{5x^3}{3y^8}$

18. Multiply $5x^3y(3xy^2 + 2x^2y^3)$.

    A. $15x^3y^2 + 10x^5y^3$
    B. $15x^3y^2 + 10x^6y^3$
    C. $15x^4y^3 + 10x^5y^4$
    D. $15x^4y^3 + 10x^6y^4$

19. Multiply $(3x + 4)(2x - 5)$.

    A. $5x^2 - 1$
    B. $6x^2 - 20$
    C. $5x^2 - 7x - 1$
    D. $6x^2 - 7x - 20$

20. Multiply $(x - 2y)(2x - y)$.

    A. $2x^2 + 2y^2$
    B. $2x^2 - 5xy + 2y^2$
    C. $2x^2 - 2y^2$
    D. $2x^2 + 5xy - 2y^2$

21. Divide $\dfrac{12p^3q - 16p^5q^2 + 10p^4q^4}{8p^2q^3}$.

    A. $\dfrac{4p}{q^2} - \dfrac{8p^3}{q} + 2p^2q$
    B. $\dfrac{4pq}{pq^2} - \dfrac{8p^3q}{pq} + \dfrac{2p^2q}{pq}$
    C. $\dfrac{3p}{2q^2} - \dfrac{2p^3}{q} + \dfrac{5p^2q}{4}$
    D. $\dfrac{3pq}{2pq^2} - \dfrac{2p^3q}{pq} + \dfrac{5p^2q}{4pq}$

22. Divide $\dfrac{21x^3 - 14x^2}{14x^3 + 21x^2}$.

    A. $\dfrac{3x - 2}{2x + 3}$
    B. $\dfrac{21x - 14}{14x + 12}$
    C. $\dfrac{3x^2 - 2x}{2x^2 + 3x}$
    D. $\dfrac{21x^2 - 14x}{14x^2 + 12x}$

23. Divide $\dfrac{9s^3t + 6st^2}{6s^3t + 4st^2}$.

    A. $\dfrac{3}{2}$

    B. $\dfrac{9}{4}$

    C. $\dfrac{9s^2 + t}{s^2 + 4t}$

    D. $\dfrac{9s^2 + 6t}{6s^2 + 4t}$

24. Divide $\dfrac{2x^2 + x - 6}{x + 2}$.

    A. $2x^2 - 3$
    B. $2x^2 - 2$
    C. $2x - 3$
    D. $2x + 5$

25. Evaluate $2x^2 - 4xy + 3y^2$ for $x = 5$ and $y = -1$.

    A. 129
    B. 73
    C. 33
    D. 27

26. Write the polynomial $6x - 2x^3 + x^4 - 7x^2 + 5$ in descending order.

27. Write "the sum of the square of a number and three less than the number" as a polynomial in x.

28. A rock dropped from a cliff has an altitude in feet given by $-16t^2 + 350$, where t is the time in seconds after the rock is released. How high is the rock 4 seconds after it is dropped?

    A. 256 feet
    B. 128 feet
    C. 94 feet
    D. 54 feet

29. What is the leading coefficient of $5x^4 - 6x^2 + 2x^6 + 1 + 7x^3 - x$?

    A. 2
    B. 4
    C. 5
    D. 7

30. Factor $12x^4y + 9x^3y^2 - 6x^2y^2$.

    A. $3x^2(4x^2y + 3xy^2 - 2y^2)$
    B. $3x^2y(4x^2 + 3xy - 2y)$
    C. $3y(4x^4 + 3x^3y - 2x^2y)$
    D. $3xy(4x^3 + 3x^2y - 2xy)$

31. Factor $3x^2 - 8x + 4$.

    A. $(x - 4)(3x - 1)$
    B. $(x - 1)(3x - 4)$
    C. $(3x - 1)(3x - 4)$
    D. $(x - 2)(3x - 2)$

32. Factor $2x^2 - xy - y^2$.

    A. $(x + y)(2x + y)$
    B. $(x - y)(2x - y)$
    C. $(x - y)(2x + y)$
    D. $(x + y)(2x - y)$

33. Factor $12x^2y + 40xy - 32y$ completely.

    A. $4y(3x - 2)(x + 4)$
    B. $4(3xy - 2y)(x + 4)$
    C. $4(3x - 2)(xy + 4y)$
    D. $(3xy - 2y)(4x + 16)$

34. Factor $16x^2 - 81y^2$.

35. Write "twice the square of a number is five more than the number" as an equation using x.

36. What is the degree of the polynomial $3x + 7x^3 - 2x^2 + 5 + 8x^4 - 6x^5$?

    A. 5
    B. 6
    C. 7
    D. 8

37. Denny leaves on a drive across the state at 8:00 a.m. In the afternoon, his average speed in miles per hour is given by $\dfrac{d}{t+4}$, where t is the number of hours past noon and d is the distance driven. Find Denny's average speed at 2:00 p.m, when he has driven 390 miles.

    A. 70 miles per hour
    B. 60 miles per hour
    C. 75 miles per hour
    D. 65 miles per hour

38. Add $\dfrac{2}{3x^2} + \dfrac{5}{6x}$. Write your answer in lowest terms.

    A. $\dfrac{4x + 5x^2}{6x^3}$
    B. $\dfrac{12 + 15x}{18x^2}$
    C. $\dfrac{4 + 5x}{6x^2}$
    D. $\dfrac{12x + 51x^2}{18x^3}$

39. Add $\dfrac{2x - 5}{5x + 10} + \dfrac{x + 1}{3x + 6}$. Write your answer in lowest terms.

    A. $\dfrac{11x - 10}{15(x + 2)^2}$
    B. $\dfrac{11x - 10}{15(x + 2)}$
    C. $\dfrac{11x^2 + 12x - 20}{(5x + 10)(3x + 6)}$
    D. $\dfrac{11x^2 + 12x - 20}{15(x + 2)^2}$

40. Subtract $\dfrac{3x}{10y} - \dfrac{4y}{15x}$. Write your answer in lowest terms.

    A. $\dfrac{9x - 8y}{15xy}$
    B. $\dfrac{9x^2 - 8y^2}{15xy}$
    C. $\dfrac{9x - 8y}{30xy}$
    D. $\dfrac{9x^2 - 8y^2}{30xy}$

41. Subtract $\dfrac{3x}{2x - 10} - \dfrac{x}{2x + 6}$. Write your answer in lowest terms.

    A. $\dfrac{4x^2 + 28x}{(2x - 10)(2x + 6)}$
    B. $\dfrac{x^2 + 14x}{(x - 5)(x + 3)}$
    C. $\dfrac{2x^2 + 14x}{2(x - 5)(x + 3)}$
    D. $\dfrac{x(x + 7)}{(x - 5)(x + 3)}$

42. Simplify $\dfrac{x + 1}{2x - 4} + \dfrac{x - 1}{2x + 4} - \dfrac{2x}{x^2 - 4}$. Write your answer in lowest terms.

    A. $\dfrac{x^2 - x + 1}{2(x - 1)(x + 1)}$
    B. $\dfrac{2x^2 - 4x + 4}{2(x - 2)(x + 2)}$
    C. $\dfrac{x^2 - 2x + 2}{(x - 2)(x + 2)}$
    D. $\dfrac{x^2 - x + 1}{(x - 1)(x + 1)}$

43. Multiply $\dfrac{3ax^4}{8b^3y} \cdot \dfrac{6b^3x^5}{9a^6y^3}$. Write your answer in lowest terms.

    A. $\dfrac{x^9}{4a^5y^4}$

    B. $\dfrac{x^{20}}{4a^6y^3}$

    C. $\dfrac{18x^{20}}{72a^6y^3}$

    D. $\dfrac{18x^9}{72a^5y^4}$

44. Multiply $\dfrac{x^2-2x-3}{x^2+3x} \cdot \dfrac{x^2-9}{x^2+2x+1}$. Write your answer in lowest terms.

    A. $\dfrac{2(x-1)(x-3)}{x(x+1)^2}$

    B. $\dfrac{(x-3)^2}{x(x+1)}$

    C. $\dfrac{2(x-3)}{x(x+1)}$

    D. $\dfrac{(x-1)(x-3)^2}{x(x+1)^2}$

45. Divide $\dfrac{20x^2y^5}{27a^6b} \div \dfrac{10b^2x^6}{9a^8y^3}$. Write your answer in lowest terms.

    A. $\dfrac{18ay^{15}}{27b^2x^3}$

    B. $\dfrac{2ay^{15}}{3b^2x^3}$

    C. $\dfrac{18a^2y^8}{27b^3x^4}$

    D. $\dfrac{2a^2y^8}{3b^3x^4}$

46. Divide $\dfrac{4x+8}{x^2+3x} \div \dfrac{x^2-4}{x^2+x-6}$. Write your answer in lowest terms.

    A. $\dfrac{4}{x}$

    B. $\dfrac{4(x+2)}{x(x-2)}$

    C. $\dfrac{4(x+2)(x-3)}{x(x+3)(x-2)}$

    D. $\dfrac{4(x+2)(x^2+x-6)}{x(x+3)(x^2-4)}$

47. Simplify $\dfrac{x^2-5x}{4x^2} \cdot \dfrac{x^2-7x+12}{x^2-16} \div \dfrac{2x-10}{x^2+2x-8}$. Write your answer in lowest terms.

    A. $\dfrac{(x+3)(x+2)}{8x}$

    B. $\dfrac{(x-3)(x+2)}{8x}$

    C. $\dfrac{(x+3)(x-2)}{8x}$

    D. $\dfrac{(x-3)(x-2)}{8x}$

48. Evaluate $\dfrac{3x^2+7x-2}{2x^2-7x+3}$ for $x = -4$.

    A. $\dfrac{74}{7}$

    B. $\dfrac{18}{7}$

    C. $\dfrac{2}{7}$

    D. 78

49. Translate into an algebraic expression using x as the variable: "the quotient of 5 more than a number and 5 less than the number."

50. After winning p dollars in a contest, June decides to donate $1000 to charity and split the rest evenly with her brother and sister. Write an expression that represents the amount June will finally have.

CHAPTER 10
Solving Equations and Inequalities

Directions: Answer the following questions. For multiple-choice questions, choose the best answer. For other questions, write your answer in the space below the question. Answers begin on page 111.

1. Solve $p - 5 = 12$.

2. Solve $7s = -56$.

3. Solve $-3x + 17 = 5$.

4. Solve $6(a - 8) = -42$.

5. Solve $5x + 2(x - 9) = 7x + 10$.

6. Gary is collecting bottlecaps to earn Chumpy credits. Each bottlecap is worth 7 Chumpy credits. Gary already has 11 bottlecaps. How many more bottlecaps does he need to have a total of 245 Chumpy credits?

7. What is the temperature in degrees Celsius if the temperature in degrees Fahrenheit is 95°F? The temperature conversion formula is
$$F = \frac{9}{5}C + 32.$$

8. Solve $y < mx + b$ for x. Assume $m > 0$.

9. Danielle is selling gift certificates at a shopping mall at the rate of 5 certificates per hour. She sold 15 certificates by noon. When will she have sold a total of 40 certificates?

10. The length of a rectangle is 5 centimeters more than the width. The perimeter of the rectangle is 90 centimeters. What is the length of the rectangle?

11. A farmer has $2000 to buy seed for his main plot. He can spend it all on milo at $50 per bag, or on soybean at $40 per bag, or some combination of the two. If m represents the number of bags of milo he buys and s the number of bags of soybean, which equation represents his spending his entire seed budget on a combination of the two types of seed?

   A. $40m + 50s = 2000$
   B. $50m + 40s = 2000$
   C. $45(m + s) = 2000$
   D. $90(m + s) = 2000$

12. A rock thrown straight up has a height given by $h = 80t - 16t^2$, where h is the height of the rock in feet and t is the time in seconds after it is released. How long will it take for the rock to strike the ground?

13. Solve $3k - 7 \geq 17$.

14. Which of the following represents the solution to $-2x - 3 < 3$?

    A.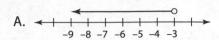

    B.

    C.

    D.

15. A passenger train leaves the station, traveling west at 120 miles per hour. A freight train leaves the same station 2 hours later traveling 80 miles per hour. If t represents the time in hours that the first train has traveled, which equation represents a situation where the two trains are 640 miles apart?

    A. $120t + 80(t - 2) = 640$
    B. $120(t + 2) + 80t = 640$
    C. $120t + 80(t + 2) = 640$
    D. $120(t - 2) + 80t = 640$

16. Solve $\begin{cases} 3x + y = 5 \\ 2x - 3y = 7 \end{cases}$.

17. Constance is controlling the flow of a solution into a graduated cylinder. She wants to go to lunch and decides to set the flow at a lower rate rather than shut it off completely. The cylinder already holds 72 milliliters of solution and can hold a maximum of 500 milliliters. If r represents the rate at which the flow is set in milliliters per minute, which inequality could Constance solve to determine a safe range of flow rates, assuming she plans to take 60 minutes for lunch?

    A. $72r + 60 \geq 500$
    B. $72r + 60 \leq 500$
    C. $60r + 72 \geq 500$
    D. $60r + 72 \leq 500$

18. Solve $4x - 2(3x + 7) = 6 + 5(x - 3)$.

19. Janie is 38 inches tall and is growing $2\frac{1}{2}$ inches per year. She wants to ride a roller-coaster, but park rules set the minimum height at 48 inches. How long must Janie wait until she can ride the roller-coaster?

20. How many pounds of peanuts worth $2.00 per pound must be mixed with cashews worth $7.00 per pound to produce 10 pounds of a mixture worth $5.00 per pound?

21. Solve $3x - 2(x - 1) = 2(x + 1) - x$.

22. Joachim has a box containing 17 red blocks, all the same size, and 13 blue blocks, all the same size. Each red block weighs r ounces, and each blue block weighs b ounces. Which equation states that all of the blocks together weigh 99 ounces?

    A. $15(r + b) = 99$
    B. $30(r + b) = 99$
    C. $13r + 17b = 99$
    D. $17r + 13b = 99$

23. Which of the following is the most reasonable constraint on the weight r of a red block?

24. Stan is diluting 5 quarts of a 50% antifreeze solution down to 20%. How much pure water should he add?

25. Write an equation that states that the surface area of a rectangular solid, of length 6, height h, and width w, is 86.

    A. $12h + 12w + 12hw = 86$
    B. $12h + 12w + 2hw = 86$
    C. $12lh + 12hw + 2hw = 86$
    D. $12h + 12w + 12 = 86$

26. Solve $x^2 - 10x - 24 = 0$.

27. Solve $\begin{cases} 6x - 5y = -8 \\ 4x + 3y = -18 \end{cases}$.

28. Which inequality has the following graph?

    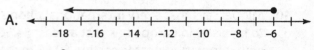

    A. $x < -2$
    B. $x \le -2$
    C. $x > -2$
    D. $x \ge -2$

29. Solve $2x + 9 > 4x - 7$.

30. Solve $\begin{cases} 3x - 5y = 2 \\ -6x + 10y = 7 \end{cases}$.

31. Jack is earning money by mowing lawns. He charges $40 per lawn. He is trying to save up at least $1500 for a new riding lawnmower. He already has $420. Which inequality best represents Jack's riding lawnmower goal?

    A. $420x + 40 \ge 1500$
    B. $40x + 420 \ge 1500$
    C. $420x + 40 \le 1500$
    D. $40x + 420 \le 1500$

32. Solve $2x^2 - 7x + 4 = 0$.

33. A square has an area of 64 square centimeters. What is the length of its sides?

34. Which graph matches $-\dfrac{2}{3}x \ge 4$?

    A. ![number line from -18 to -6, arrow pointing left with closed circle at -6]
    B. ![number line from -6 to 6, arrow pointing right with closed circle at -6]
    C. ![number line from 4 to 12, arrow pointing right with closed circle at 4]
    D. ![number line from -4 to 4, arrow pointing left with closed circle at 4]

35. Solve $x^2 = 25$.

36. The length of a rectangle is 4 units longer than the width, and the area is 45 square units. What are the dimensions of the rectangle?

37. A strong solution of 90% detergent is being mixed with a weak solution of 15% detergent in order to produce a mild solution of 50% detergent. How much of each of the two detergents should be mixed in order to produce 60 gallons of the mild detergent?

38. Solve $7x - 6 \le 2x + 4$.

39. Which graph matches the inequality $x \leq 0$?

    A.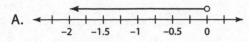

    B.

    C.

    D.

40. Miguel says that every international phone call to his sister in Europe has cost at least $4.50, with international rates costing $0.65 to make the connection and $0.35 per minute. Which inequality represents the number of minutes m that Miguel talks to his sister for each call?

    A. $m \geq 11$
    B. $m \geq 12$
    C. $m \geq 14$
    D. $m \geq 15$

41. To which of the following inequalities is the number 11 a solution?

    A. $3x - 5 < 2(2 - x)$
    B. $7x - 3 \geq 7 - 3x$
    C. $5(x - 2) \leq 3(x + 1)$
    D. $4(x - 8) > 2x + 5$

42. Solve $ax + by = c$ for y.

43. As a goodwill gesture, Florence is giving $5 to each person who participates in a public cleanup program. She started with $400. After two hours, she had already given away $135. Which inequality represents the number of people she can still give $5 to?

    A. $p \leq 51$
    B. $p \leq 52$
    C. $p \leq 53$
    D. $p \leq 54$

44. Which graph matches $x + 19 < 15$?

    A.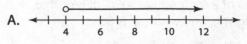

    B.

    C.

    D.

45. Solve $2x - 4(x + 3) \geq 4 + 3(4 - 3x)$.

46. Amy makes a gas stop at a station where gas is selling at $3.15 per gallon, including taxes. While there, she buys a bottle of water for $1.65. Her total is $40.71. If Amy bought g gallons of gas, which equation models Amy's purchase?

    A. $1.64g + 3.15 = 40.71$
    B. $1.65g + 40.71 = 3.15$
    C. $3.15g + 1.65 = 40.71$
    D. $3.15g + 40.71 = 1.65$

47. Sean earns $5 for every order he fills at a call-in center, plus base pay of $150 per week. During a week in which he earns $580, how many orders does he fill?

48. Solve $5(x - 6) < 2(x - 9)$.

49. Solve $2x^2 - 7x + 6 = 0$.

50. A rock dropped from a 1024-foot-high cliff falls a distance D given by $D = 16t^2$, where t is the time in seconds after the rock is dropped. How long will it take the rock to reach the bottom of the cliff?

CHAPTER 11

Graphing Equations

Directions: Answer the following questions. For multiple-choice questions, choose the best answer. For other questions, write your answer in the space below the question. Answers begin on page 115.

1. For the following, place the letter of the coordinates on the appropriate point on the graph.

   A. (9, 15)
   B. (5, 5)
   C. (10, 1)
   D. (0, 0)
   E. (10, −1)
   F. (−5, 5)
   G. (−5, −5)
   H. (−2, −10)
   I. (−8, −2)
   J. (5, −5)
   K. Coordinates not listed (may be used more than once)

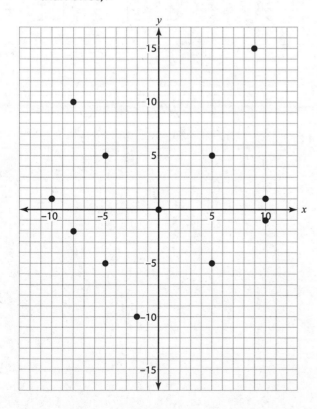

2. In the box associated with each line, place the correct slope. [Choices: $-\frac{7}{3}$, $-\frac{1}{3}$, 0, $\frac{1}{10}$, 2, undefined]

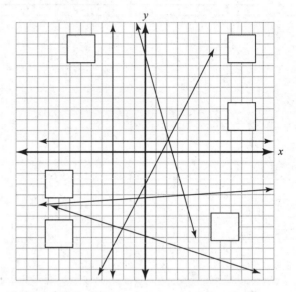

3. Given a line whose equation is $y = -\frac{1}{4}x + 7$, which line below definitely forms part of a right triangle with the given line?

   A. $y = \frac{1}{4}x + 9$

   B. $y = -4x + 7$

   C. $y = -\frac{1}{4}x + 5$

   D. $y = 4x + 11$

4. A point on the line $4x + 3y = b$ is (3, 2). What is the y coordinate for $x = 4$?

5. Which graph shows the proper end behavior for the equation $y = x^3 + 2x^2$ as x becomes a large positive or negative number?

A.
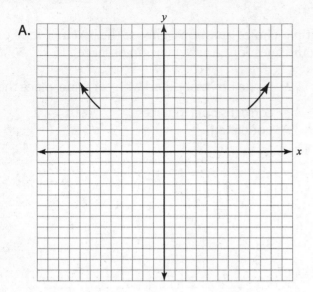

C.
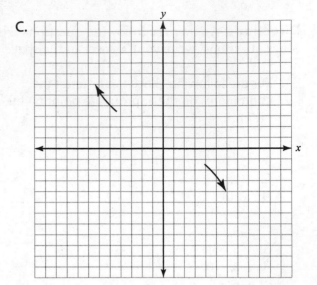

B.
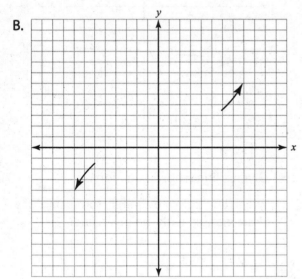

D.
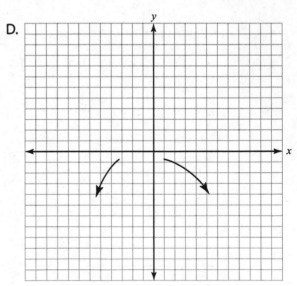

6. Which of the four curves in this graphic is that of $y = -\dfrac{4}{5}x + 3$?

A.

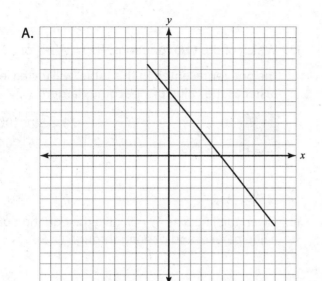

C.

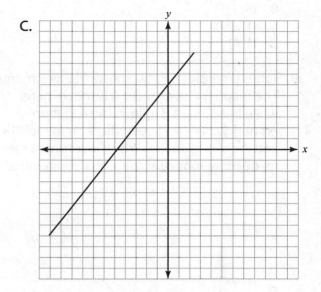

B.

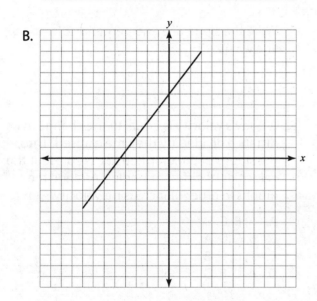

D.

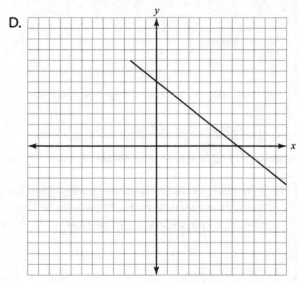

7. Which of the following points is on the line $y = 7x - 4$?

   A. (7, 3)
   B. (5, 31)
   C. (11, 72)
   D. (1, 4)

8. Jones is considering two possible investments. The graph for Investment A is shown here, while Investment B follows the equation Profit = $2,500t - $1,000, where t is in months and Profit is in dollars. Which investment has made more money at the end of six months?

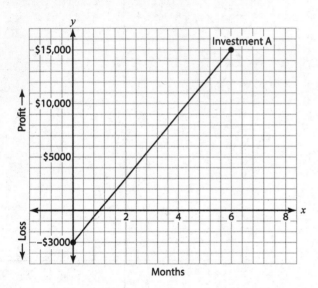

Months

9. If Jones is going to hold the investment longer than six months, which of the ones in the previous question should he buy?

10. A particular curve passes through the points (11, 8), (-3, -6), and (4, 2). Are these points on

   the graph of a linear function? Check _____ Yes

   or _____ No.

11. What is the equation for a straight line passing through (-3, 5) and (5, -3)?

12. What is the equation for a line perpendicular to $6x - 7y = 8$ and passing through the point (8, 1)?

13. Which of the two functions, $f(x) = \dfrac{x^3}{x - 2}$ or the one represented in this table, will increase faster as the value of x becomes larger?

x	0	1	2	3	4	20	50	100
$f(x)$	4	6	8	10	12	44	104	204

14. Given the line $5x - 4y = 9$, give the equation of a line parallel and passing through (9, 5).

15. Write the slope of a line perpendicular to the line $y = 4x - 7$.

16. A body's velocity is equal to the change in its distance divided by the time elapsed. Thus, the slopes of the graphed lines represent the velocities of different bodies. Arrange the graphs in order of increasing velocity.

   A. A, B, C, D
   B. B, C, D, A
   C. A, D, C, B
   D. A, C, B, D

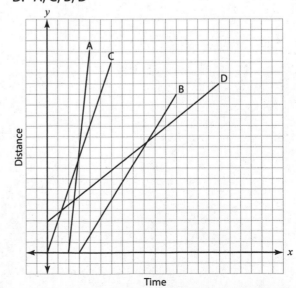

Time

17. On the time-distance graph, what is the meaning of a line that has a negative slope?

    A. The body is moving backward.
    B. The body is slowing down.
    C. The body is stationary.
    D. Nothing. Velocities, like distances, can't be negative.

18. A body moves according to the equation $d = vt$, where v is velocity, t is time, and d is distance. If a given body moves 250 meters in 10 seconds, is it going faster or slower than the body represented on this graph?

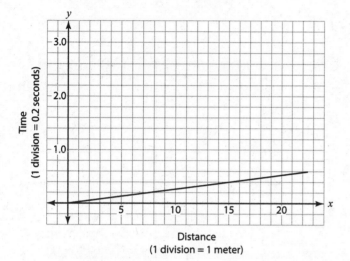

Distance
(1 division = 1 meter)

    A. It is moving more slowly than the body in the graph.
    B. It is moving faster than the body in the graph.
    C. Both are moving at the same speed.
    D. Neither is actually moving.

19. Which of the equations below is that of a line with slope of $\frac{3}{5}$ and passing through (0, 4)?

    A. $2x - 3y = 6$
    B. $5y - 3x = 20$
    C. $5y - 3x = 4$
    D. $5y - 3x = 2$

20. Graph the following function, using open circles for points on the ends of lines that are not in the solution set, and solid points for those that are.

    $y = x + 2 \qquad x \le -4$

    $y = \frac{1}{4}x^2 \qquad -4 < x < 0$

    $y = \frac{6}{25}x^2 \qquad 0 \le x \le 5$

    $y = -2x + 6 \qquad x > 5$

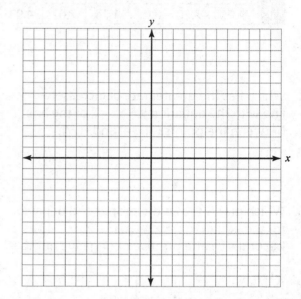

21. In this diagram, what is the slope of line A?

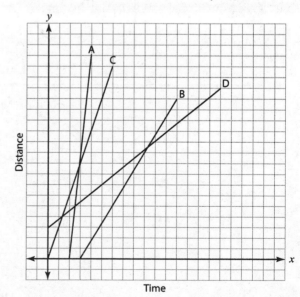

22. Write the second order equation for a curve passing through a vertex at (1, 5) and passing through (0, 8).

23. Given the table of values below, write a linear function that approximates the relationship between x and y.

x	−2.07	−1.02	0.001	0.50	1.00	1.95
y	−4.00	−2.20	−0.01	1.04	2.02	4.03

24. Which has the greater rate of increase, a line with the equation $y = 5x - 7$ or the line between the points (−1, −4) and (1, 7)?

25. Which graph shows the proper end behavior for the equation $y = x^4 + 35x^3 - 23x^2 - 43$ as x becomes a large positive or negative number?

A.

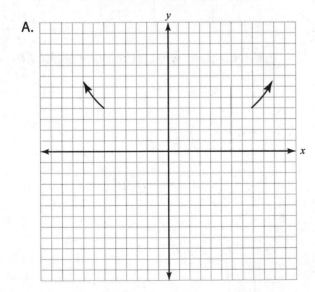

B.

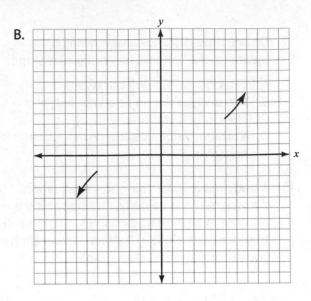

C.

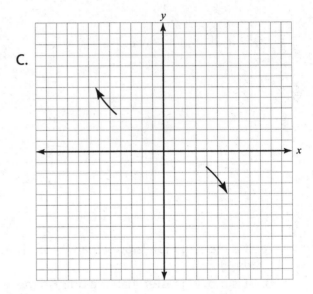

D.

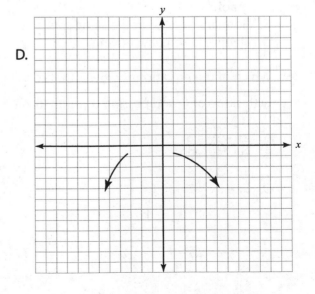

26. A road rises 4 feet over the course of 100 horizontal feet. What is the slope of a line representing the road?

    A. 4
    B. 0.04
    C. 2.5
    D. 25

27. Plot the curve for $f(x) = \dfrac{1}{x^2}$ and label any asymptotes.

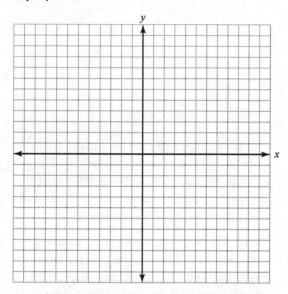

28. Graph the equation $y = -5x^2 + 35x$, and estimate and label the maximum value of y.

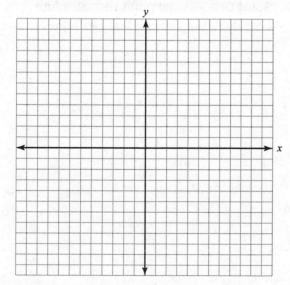

29. Write the equation of a line passing through the points (3, 7) and (2, −4).

30. Claire goes to a used bookstore in search of novels and biographies, She spends a total of $24, buying b biographies for $3 each and n novels for $4 each. Write an equation relating the numbers of each type of book Claire bought. Graph your equation, putting b on the horizontal axis.

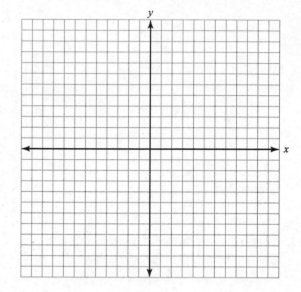

31. Plot the graph of $y = |3x|$.

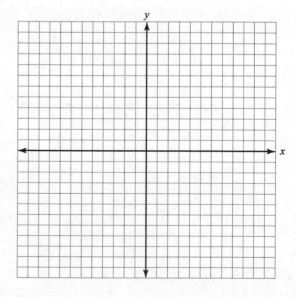

32. The equation relating the number of customized cell phones produced and the profit per cell phone is $p = -2.50n^2 + 21n$, where n is in 100,000s. Plot the resulting graph. Be sure to label and number the axes appropriately and indicate the maximum value of p.

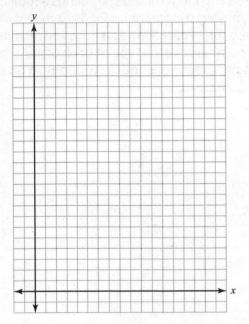

33. Graph the equation of a straight line that passes through $(-1, 3)$ and has a slope of -3.

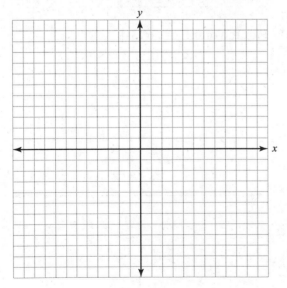

34. Graph the equation $5x - 4y = -20$.

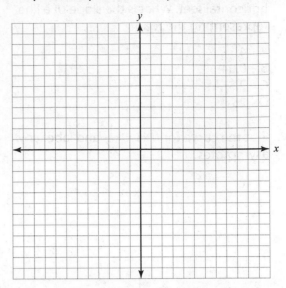

35. The coordinates of four points are given in absolute terms (all values positive). Plot and label each point in the quadrant requested. Different quadrants will require changing the signs of some or all the coordinates.

Point A: Plot the point with absolute coordinates of $(3, 6)$ in the third quadrant.
Point B: Plot the point with absolute coordinates of $(5, 5)$ in the second quadrant.
Point C: Plot the point with absolute coordinates of $(2, 7)$ in the third quadrant.
Point D: Plot the point with absolute coordinates of $(5, 9)$ in the fourth quadrant.

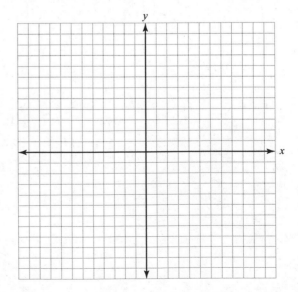

36. Two rockets are launched, one of which follows the trajectory shown here. The elevation of the other rocket follows the equation $e(t) = -100t^2 + 1200t$, where e equals feet of elevation and t equals seconds in flight. Which rocket climbs to a greater height?

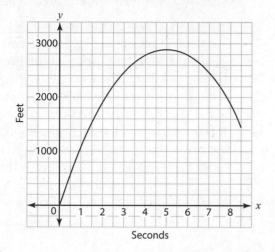

37. Which graph shows the proper end behavior for the equation $y = 4x^2 - 2x$ as x becomes a large positive or negative number?

A.

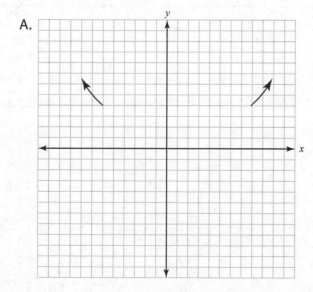

B.

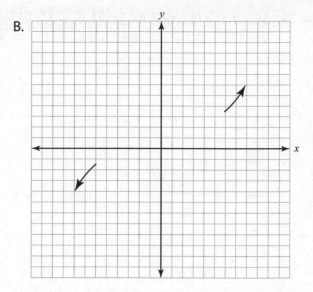

C.

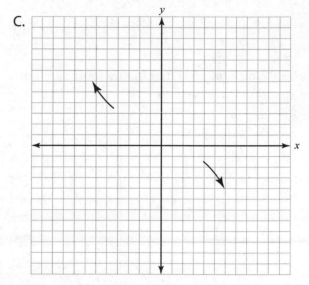

D.

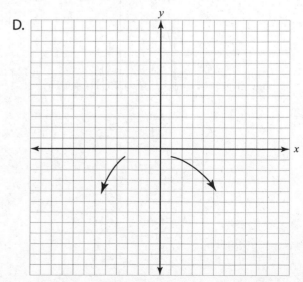

38. Sketch the function $f(x) = x^2 + 6x + 8$, and list the intercepts, if any, with the x and $f(x)$ axes.

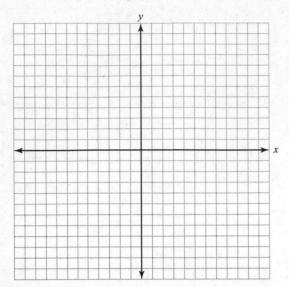

B.

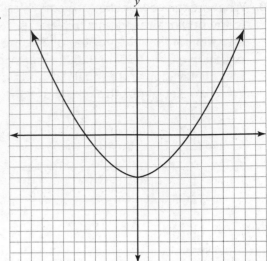

39. Which graph(s) that follow show symmetry with the x-axis?

A.

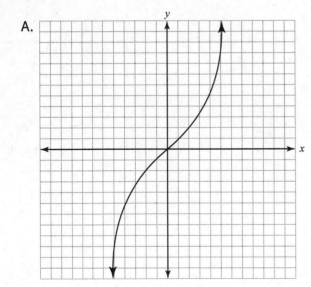

C.

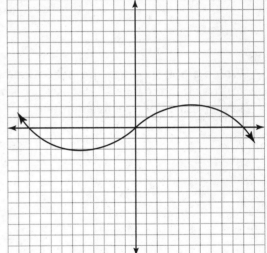

D.

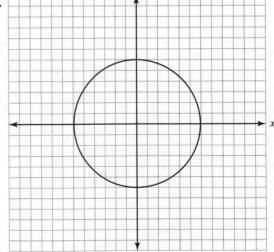

40. What are the coordinates of a point symmetric to the origin with the point (3, –9)?

41. What are the end behaviors of
$y = 3x^3 + 15x^2 - 6x + 5$?

    A. +∞ for $x < 0$ and −∞ for $x > 0$
    B. −∞ for $x < 0$ and −∞ for $x > 0$
    C. −∞ for $x < 0$ and +∞ for $x > 0$
    D. +∞ for $x < 0$ and +∞ for $x > 0$

42. Which of the following graph(s) does NOT show symmetry with the *y*-axis?

A.

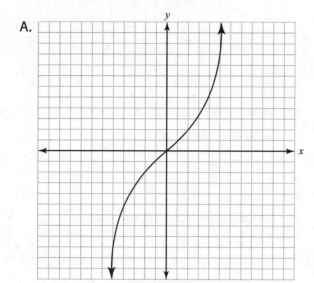

B.

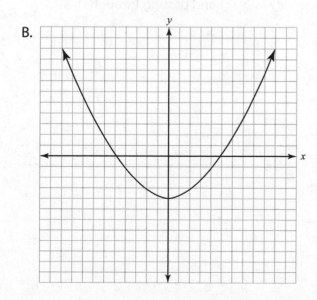

C.

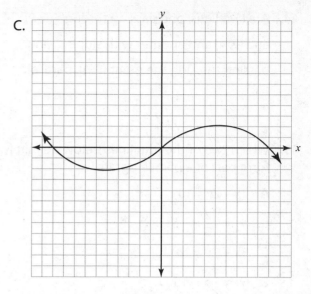

D.

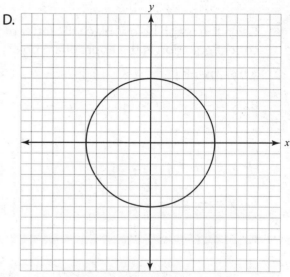

43. What is the slope of line B in the diagram below?

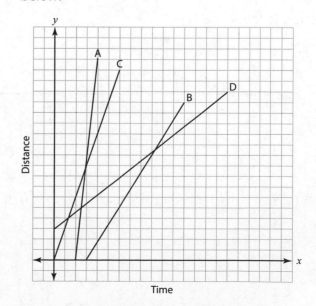

44. Are two lines, one passing through (6, 9) and (2, 4) and another with slope $\frac{5}{4}$ and passing through the point (2, 1), parallel?

45. Which two of the four lines below definitely form part of a parallelogram?

    A. $3x - 2y = 10$

    B. $y = -\frac{2}{3}x - 5$

    C. $3x + 2y = 10$

    D. $y = \frac{3}{2}x - 15$

46. Given the graph below, place the letter of the correct equation in the appropriate box.

    A. $y = 2x + 11$

    B. $y = \frac{1}{2}x + 10$

    C. $y = x^3 + 5$

    D. $y = \frac{3}{4}x + \frac{1}{2}$

    E. $y = -\frac{2}{3}x + \frac{1}{2}$

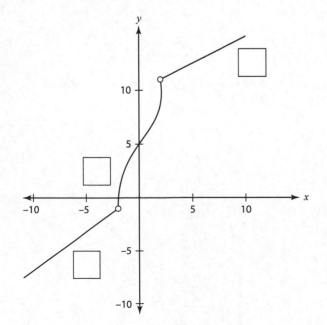

47. Given the equation $y = -2x^2 + 5$, graph the equation so that the maxima or minima intercepts with the x-axis and end behaviors are evident.

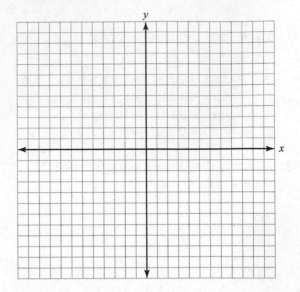

48. What is the equation of a line passing through (4, 5) with slope $-\frac{2}{3}$?

49. Where is the intersection of a line perpendicular to $y = -\frac{2}{3}x + 5$ and passing through (–2, –2) and a second line parallel to $y = -x + 1$ and passing through (1, 5)?

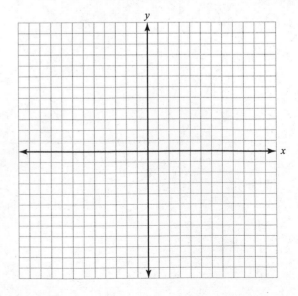

50. Which graph shows the proper end behaviors
    for the equation $y = -x^2 + 7x - 7$?

A.

B.

C.

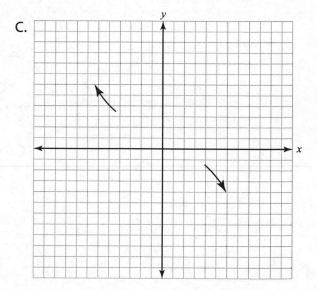

D.

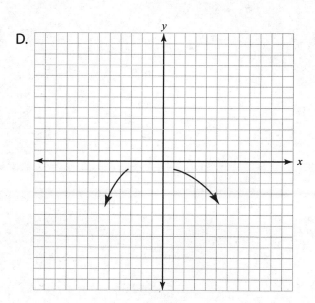

CHAPTER 12

Functions

Directions: Answer the following questions. For multiple-choice questions, choose the best answer. For other questions, write your answer in the space below the question. Answers begin on page 120.

1. Graph $y = \dfrac{3}{2}x$.

3. Which of the functions has the larger positive x-intercept, the function graphed here or the function given by the equation $y = -7x + 24$?

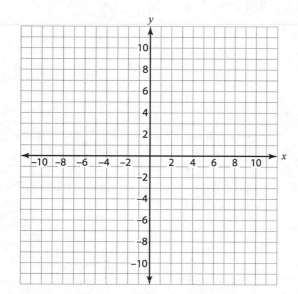

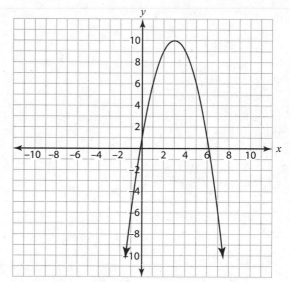

2. Which of the tables of input-output pairs, where x represents the input and y the output, does NOT represent a function?

A.

x	3	2	7	3	8	2
y	9	4	1	9	2	4

B.

x	1	2	4	7	8	9
y	4	8	2	7	1	5

C.

x	1	4	6	4	3	1
y	2	3	8	7	6	2

D.

x	5	8	2	4	2	5
y	0	0	0	3	0	0

4. Which of the following implicitly defines a linear function?

A. $x^2 + y^2 = 25$

B. $3x - 5y = 9$

C. $y = \dfrac{1}{3x} - 2$

D. $xy = 8$

5. Where is the function in the graph increasing?

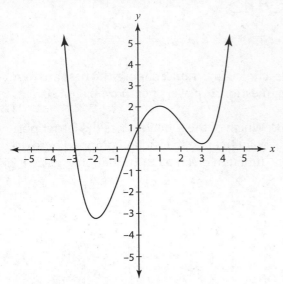

A. $-2 < x < 1$ and $x > 3$
B. $x < -2$ and $x > 3$
C. $x < -2$ and $1 < x < 3$
D. everywhere

6. Which function assigns the domain value 12 to the range value 7?

A. $f(x) = 2x - 2$
B. $f(x) = 3x - 4$
C. $f(x) = \frac{1}{2}x + 1$
D. $f(x) = \frac{3}{7}x + 12$

7. For $f(x) = \frac{2}{5}x + \frac{4}{5}$, find $f(-7)$.

8. A function is being used by the manager of a factory producing lawn mowers. The output of the function tells the manager how many lawn mowers will be made, using the number of workers for the input. What types of numbers are acceptable values for the input?

A. Any number will do.
B. Only positive numbers can be used.
C. Only integers can be used.
D. Only non-negative integers can be used.

9. A function is given by $f(x) = -2x + 10$. Another function is graphed here. Which function has the larger initial value?

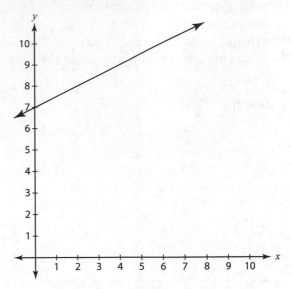

10. Describe the symmetry displayed by the graph.

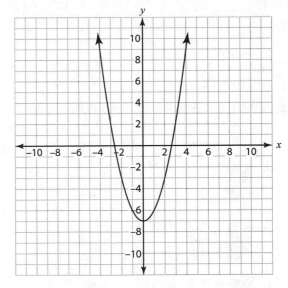

A. symmetric about the x-axis
B. symmetric about the y-axis
C. symmetric about the origin
D. no symmetry

11. Which equation does NOT implicitly define a linear function?

A. $y = x^2 + 5$
B. $y = 3x + 2$
C. $4x - 6y = 11$
D. $y + 3 = -2(x - 5)$

12. A function $d(t)$ is being used to predict the distance a bird flies t hours after release from a wildlife rehab program. What numbers are acceptable domain values?

    A. any number will do
    B. only positive numbers
    C. only integers
    D. only non-negative numbers

13. The graph shows the distance of a freight train moving away from the center of a large city. A taxi is moving away from the center of the same city, with distance determined by the function $f(t) = 40t + 5$. Which vehicle is moving faster?

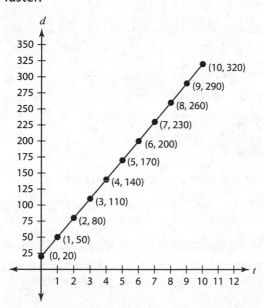

14. Find two ordered pairs (x, y) that illustrate why the equation $y^2 = x$ does not represent a function.

15. Graph $f(x) = -\dfrac{3}{2}x + 8$.

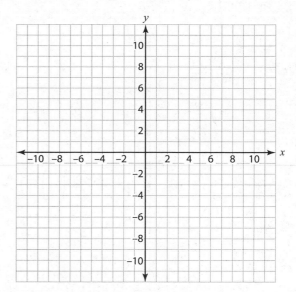

16. Find $f(-3)$ for $f(x) = -2x^2 - 7x + 9$.

17. A linear function $f(x)$ is specified by the values in the table. Another is given by $g(x) = -3x + 5$. Which function has the larger slope?

x	−2	0	3	5	9
$f(x)$	−7	−3	3	7	15

18. Which of the functions, $g(x)$ given in the graph or $f(x) = x^2 - 8x + 8$, has the larger minimum value?

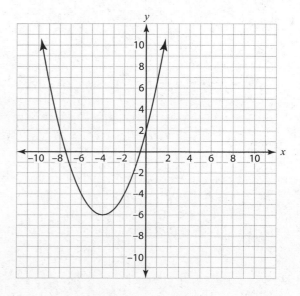

19. Which type of symmetry is NOT exhibited by this graph?

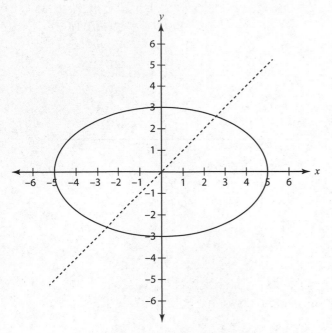

   A. symmetry about the x-axis
   B. symmetry about the y-axis
   C. symmetry about the origin
   D. symmetry about the diagonal $y = x$

20. Sketch the quadratic function that has a maximum at (3, 6) and passes through (7, 2) and (−3, −3).

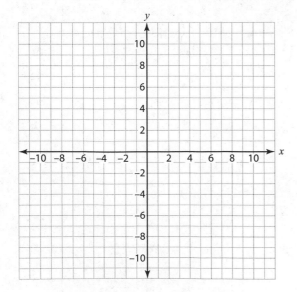

21. Write the domain of the function in the graph as an inequality.

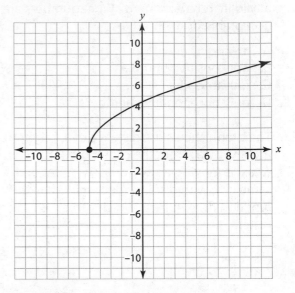

22. Fill in the missing value in the table so that the pairs represent a function.

x	7	−3	−2	4	−3
y	4	8	−1	−4	

23. An accountant uses the function

   $R(v) = \dfrac{2000}{v + 100}$ to predict the pattern of

   return of a particular investment, where R is the return, expressed as a percentage, and v is the dollar value invested. What return can she expect from an investment of $400?

24. Kenny and Jimmy have a footrace. Jimmy's distance in feet from the starting line after t seconds is given by $J(t) = 3.95t$. Kenny's distance in feet from the starting line after t seconds during the race is in the table. Assuming they both keep a constant pace, who wins the race?

t	5	10	15	20	25	30	35	40	45
K(t)	19.5	39	58.5	78	97.5	117	136.5	156	175.5

25. The graph of $f(x)$, as shown here, has two x-intercepts. The graph of $g(x) = x^2 - 2x + 1$ has only one. Which of the following statements is true?

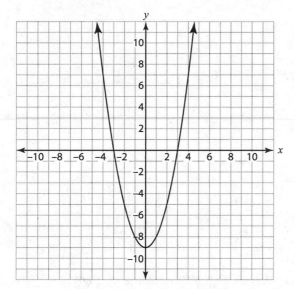

A. The x-intercept of $g(x)$ lies between those of $f(x)$.
B. The x-intercept of $g(x)$ lies to the right of those of $f(x)$.
C. The x-intercept of $g(x)$ lies to the left of those of $f(x)$.
D. The x-intercept of $g(x)$ coincides with one of those of $f(x)$.

26. Evaluate $f(x) = \dfrac{5}{9}x^2 - \dfrac{2}{3}x - 7$ for $x = -6$.

27. A sand hopper is emptied through a chute. The amount w of sand in kilograms t seconds after the chute is opened is given by $w(t) = 1000 - 5t$. The hopper next to it is being filled from a dump truck. The truck's entire load of 125 kilograms of sand is dumped in 30 seconds. Which is moving sand faster, the open chute or the truck while dumping?

28. A tool factory manager is evaluating two machines that stamp parts for hammers. The result of his testing is displayed in the graph. Which machine should the factory buy?

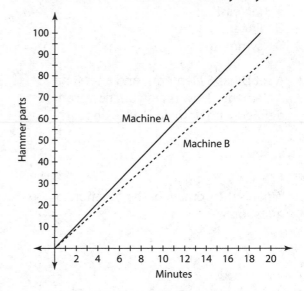

29. Graph the function given in the following table.

x	−7	−6	−3	−1	0	2	5	6	8
f(x)	4	−1	0	7	−2	6	2	−4	1

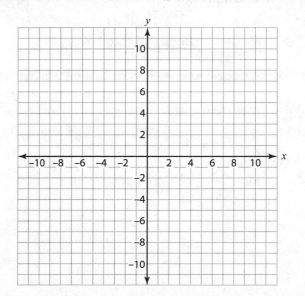

30. A line passes through the point (0, 17) on the y-axis and continues to the right, dropping 3 units for every unit to the right. A second line is given by $5x - 3y = 30$. Which line has the larger x-intercept, the first or the second?

31. What word best describes the function
    $f(x) = -\frac{4}{13}x - \frac{7}{5}$?

    A. negative
    B. increasing
    C. linear
    D. symmetric

32. A set D has 5 elements, and a set R has 3 elements. How many functions can be defined with domain D and range R?

33. What is the domain of the function in question 29?

34. The function $I(n) = 28,000 + 4,000n$ represents the average annual income in dollars for a person with n years of college education. What is the best interpretation for the equation $I(4) = 44,000$?

    A. A person with 4 years of college should request an annual average salary of $44,000 when interviewing.
    B. A person with 4 years of college will earn $44,000 more each year on average than if they didn't attend college.
    C. A person with 4 years of college will earn $44,000 annually, on average.
    D. A person with 4 years of college should look for a position that starts at $44,000 annually.

35. Where is the function in the graph below constant?

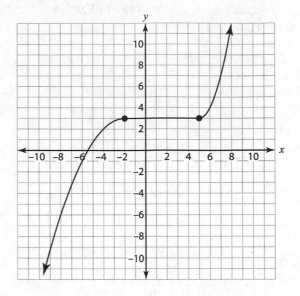

36. Which is steeper, the line $g(x)$ whose x-intercept is 7 and y-intercept is –5, or the linear function $f(x) = -3x + 9$?

37. Luz built a function $h(t) = -16t^2 + 320t$ to estimate the height in feet of an object launched vertically from the ground t seconds after launch. The object she launches carries a miniaturized telemetry broadcaster, from which she records the data in the table below during a test launch. Does the function predict the object's falling to the ground sooner or later than is indicated by the telemetry?

t	3	6	9	12	15
$T(t)$	576	864	864	576	0

38. The equation $f(a) = b$ implies that what point is on the graph of $f(x)$?

39. Where is the function $f(x) = \frac{5}{8}x - \frac{25}{16}$ negative?

40. Where is the function in the graph positive?

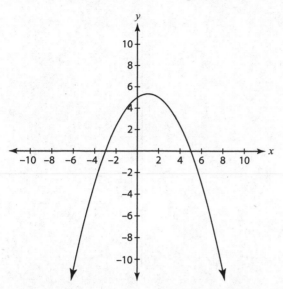

41. The following table displays values in a proportional relationship. The graph that follows displays a different proportional relationship. Which relationship has the larger rate of change?

x	3	5	8	12
P(x)	54	90	144	216

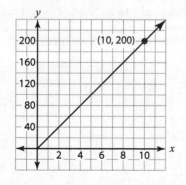

42. Is the following graph that of a function? Why, or why not?

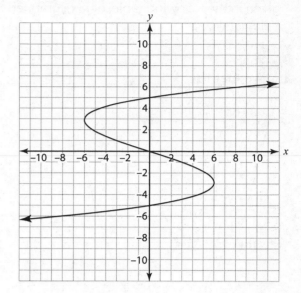

43. Evaluate $f\left(-\dfrac{3}{2}\right)$ for $f(x) = 4x^2 - 6x + 3$.

44. What is the domain of the function in the following graph?

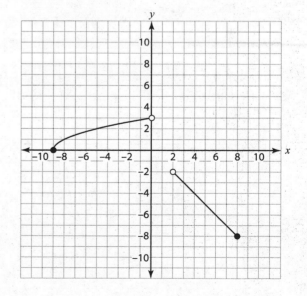

45. Which quadratic function is negative over a larger subset of its domain, $f(x)$, with values given in the following table, or $g(x)$, graphed below?

x	−5	−4	−1	0	3	4	7	8
f(x)	3	0	−6	−7	−7	−6	0	3

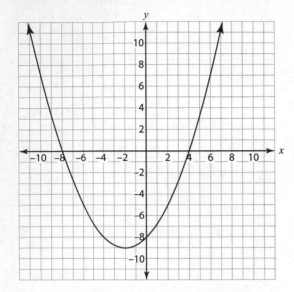

46. Is the following graph that of a function? Why or why not?

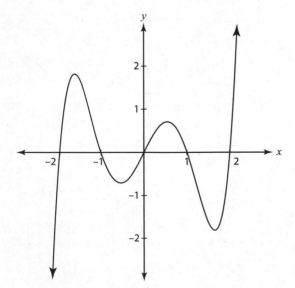

47. Which of the intercepts of $f(x) = -\dfrac{9}{10}x + 9$ is closer to the origin?

48. Graph $f(x) = x^2 - 4x - 5$.

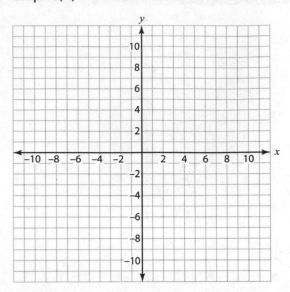

49. A baseball is hit by the batter; its height in feet t seconds after being hit is given by $h(t) = -16t^2 + 128t + 4$. What is the maximum height of the ball, reached 4 seconds after being hit?

50. What is the domain of the baseball height function in question 49?

Chapter 1 Whole Numbers and Integers

1.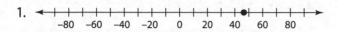

   47 is closer to 50 than to 40.

2.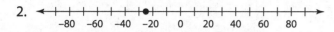

   −25 is negative, so it is to the left of 0.

3. < Any negative number is less than any positive number.

4. < −47 is farther to the left than −44.

5. > Any positive number is greater than any negative number.

6. D −(−5) = 5

7. B The opposite of the opposite of a number is the same number.

8. A The vertical bars indicate absolute value.

9. D Absolute value is the distance from 0, which is always positive.

10. D Positive x values are to the right; negative y values are below the x-axis.

11. C Quadrants are named counter-clockwise, starting in the upper right. Quadrant III is to the left of the y-axis and below the x-axis.

12. A Reflections in the x-axis change the sign of the y value.

13. B Reflections in the x-axis change the sign of the y value.

14. D Reflections in the y-axis change the sign of the x value.

15. C Changing the sign of 0 does not affect its value.

16. D (−3, 2): 3 units left and 2 units up

17. B (4, −5): 4 units right, 5 units down

18. B −3 is a larger number than −7 and so is to its right.

19. B Death Valley is not as far below sea level as the Dead Sea is.

20. D The absolute value of a number is the distance of the number from 0.

21. B All statements are true, but in geometric terms, "<" means "is to the left of."

22. D They all have a debt equal to the absolute value of their balance.

23. B factors of 42: 1, 2, 3, 6, 7, 14, 21, 42
    factors of 36: 1, 2, 3, 4, 6 , 9, 12, 18, 36
    common factors: 1, 2, 3, 6
    largest of these: 6

24. B multiples of 6: 6, 12, 18, 24, 30, 36, 42, 48, . . .
    multiples of 9: 9, 18, 27, 36, 45, . . .
    common multiples: 18, 36, . . .
    smallest of these: 18

25. B from the friend's point of view, −85 + 5(17) = −85 + 85 = 0

26. D Adding a negative is a move to the left on the number line.

27. B Number + opposite starts at zero, goes to the number, and then returns.

28. B 3 − 7 = 3 + (−7) = −4

29. D 5 − (−6) = 5 + 6 = 11

30. A 7 + (−5) + (−9) = 2 + (−9) = −7

31. C −3 − (−8) + (−4) − 5 = −3 + 8 + (−4) + (−5) = 5 + (−4) + (−5) = 1 + (−5) = −4

32. C −9 + 3 + (−4) = −6 + (−4) = −10

33. A −8 − (−10) − 5 = −8 + 10 + (−5) = 2 + (−5) = −3

34. C The product of two numbers with identical signs is positive.

35. B 2(−4)(−1) = (−8)(−1) = 8

36. C The quotient of two numbers with different signs is negative.

37. **A** The quotient of two numbers with different signs is negative.

38. **A** The quotient of two numbers with identical signs is positive.

39. **C** $-20 \div (-4) = 5$

40. **D** The distance between two numbers is the absolute value of their difference (as opposed to the difference of their absolute values, as in C, or any sum, as in A and B).

41.

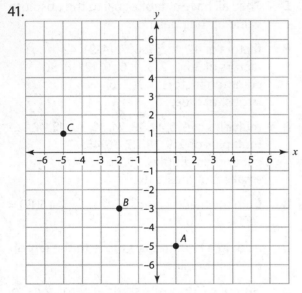

Negative x values are left of the y-axis.
Positive x values are right of the y-axis.
Negative y values are below the x-axis.
Positive y values are above the x-axis.

42. **C** $-17 - (-52) = -17 + 52 = 35$

43. **B** Division by 0 is undefined; there is no need to compute any of the numerators.

44. **–20, –15, –8, –2, 0, 6, 13**

The negative number with largest absolute value is the smallest in the group, so it is first.

45. **D** $|-7 - 6| = |-7 + (-6)| = |-13| = 13$
Distance must be positive.

46. **0** This is the only number equal to its own opposite.

47. **C** Start at 0, follow arrow to 5, back up (negative) 8, end up at –3.

48. **A** Start at 0, go left 6, then right 2, gives the addition problem $-6 + 2$. As a subtraction problem, this would have been changed from $-6 - (-2)$, ending up at –4.

49. **B** $-40(9) = -360; -360 + 160 = -200;$
$-200 \div 5 = -40$

50. **D** $-7(-5) - 4(-8 - 6) \div (-2) =$
$35 - 4(-8 + (-6)) \div (-2) =$
$35 - 4(-14) \div (-2) =$
$35 - (-56) \div (-2) =$
$35 - 28 = 7$

Chapter 2 Exponents, Roots, and Properties of Numbers

1. **C** The number of factors is the power.

2. **B** The power is the number of factors.

3. **A** The number of factors is the power.

4. **C** $4^3 = 4 \cdot 4 \cdot 4 = 16 \cdot 4 = 64$

5. **A** The base is the quantity to which the exponent is attached.

6. **C** $5^3 = 5 \cdot 5 \cdot 5 = 25 \cdot 5 = 125$

7. **D** $9^5 \cdot 9^3 = 9^{5+3} = 9^8$

ANSWERS AND SOLUTIONS

8. **D** $\quad 4^6 \cdot 2^6 = (4 \cdot 2)^6 = 8^6$

9. **A** $\quad 2^5 \cdot 3^5 \cdot 6^7 = (2 \cdot 3)^5 \cdot 6^7 = 6^5 \cdot 6^7 = 6^{5+7} = 6^{12}$

10. **B** $\quad 7^3 \cdot 7^2 \cdot 7^5 = 7^{3+2+5} = 7^{10}$

11. **C** $\quad 2^3 \cdot 4^3 \cdot 5^3 = (2 \cdot 4 \cdot 5)^3 = 40^3$

12. **B** $\quad$ Any non-zero number to the zero power is 1.

13. **D** $\quad (5^3)^4 = 5^{3 \cdot 4} = 5^{12}$

14. **C** $\quad$ Any number to the first power is that number.

15. **B** $\quad 3 \cdot 3^3 = 3^1 \cdot 3^3 = 3^{1+3} = 3^4$

16. **A** $\quad 6^5(6^2)^3 = 6^5 \cdot 6^{2 \cdot 3} = 6^5 \cdot 6^6 = 6^{5+6} = 6^{11}$

17. **D** $\quad (3^5)^2(3^4)^3 = 3^{5 \cdot 2} \cdot 3^{4 \cdot 3} = 3^{10} \cdot 3^{12} = 3^{10+12} = 3^{22}$

18. **A** $\quad 5^{-2} = \dfrac{1}{5^2} = \dfrac{1}{25}$

19. **C** $\quad (2^{-3})^2 = 2^{-3 \cdot 2} = 2^{-6} = \dfrac{1}{2^6} = \dfrac{1}{64}$

20. **B** $\quad (5^{-2})^{-4} = 5^{-2 \cdot (-4)} = 5^8$

21. **B** $\quad$ 10 to the 5th is 1 followed by 5 zeroes.

22. **D** $\quad$ 1 to any power is 1.

23. **A** $\quad 2^4 \cdot 2^{-9} = 2^{4+(-9)} = 2^{-5} = \dfrac{1}{2^5} = \dfrac{1}{32}$

24. **A** $\quad \dfrac{3^7}{3^5} = 3^{7-5} = 3^2 = 3 \cdot 3 = 9$

25. **C** $\quad \dfrac{5^3}{5^6} = 5^{3-6} = 5^{3+(-6)} = 5^{-3} = \dfrac{1}{5^3} = \dfrac{1}{125}$

26. **B** $\quad 10^{-2} = \dfrac{1}{10^2} = \dfrac{1}{100}$

27. **A** $\quad$ 0 to any positive power is 0.

28. **D** $\quad \left(\dfrac{7}{8}\right)^5 = \dfrac{7^5}{8^5}$

29. **B** $\quad \left(\dfrac{2}{3}\right)^4 = \dfrac{2^4}{3^4} = \dfrac{16}{81}$

30. **C** $\quad 2^6 \cdot 5^6 = (2 \cdot 5)^6 = 10^6 = 1,000,000$

31. **D** $\quad (5^4 \cdot 7^9)^3 = (5^4)^3 \cdot (7^9)^3 = 5^{4 \cdot 3} \cdot 7^{9 \cdot 3} = 5^{12} \cdot 7^{27}$

32. **B** $\quad 100^{\frac{1}{2}} = \sqrt{100} = 10$

33. **A** $\quad 8^{\frac{1}{3}} = \sqrt[3]{8} = 2$

34. **C** $\quad 25^{-\frac{1}{2}} = \dfrac{1}{25^{\frac{1}{2}}} = \dfrac{1}{\sqrt{25}} = \dfrac{1}{5}$

35. **B** $\quad 1000^{-\frac{1}{3}} = \dfrac{1}{1000^{\frac{1}{3}}} = \dfrac{1}{\sqrt[3]{1000}} = \dfrac{1}{10}$

36. **A** $\quad 4^{2^{-1}} = 4^{\frac{1}{2}} = \sqrt{4} = 2$

37. **D** $\quad$ by definition

38. **B** $\quad$ by definition

39. **C** $\quad$ by definition

40. **A** $\quad$ by definition

41. **C** $\quad 9^2 = 9 \cdot 9 = 81$

42. **B** $\quad 6^2 = 6 \cdot 6 = 36$

43. **D** $\quad 4^3 = 4 \cdot 4 \cdot 4 = 16 \cdot 4 = 64$

44. **A** $\quad 3^3 = 3 \cdot 3 \cdot 3 = 9 \cdot 3 = 27$

45. **D** $\quad 54 - 30 = 6 \cdot 9 - 6 \cdot 5 = 6(9 - 5)$

46. **A** $\quad 5(7 + 2) = 5 \cdot 7 + 5 \cdot 2 = 35 + 10$

47. **C** $\quad 3(9 - 5) = 3 \cdot 9 - 3 \cdot 5 = 27 - 15$

48. **B** $\quad 64 + 28 = 4 \cdot 16 + 4 \cdot 7 = 4(16 + 7)$

49. **D** $\quad 2(3 + 5 - 4) = 2 \cdot 3 + 2 \cdot 5 - 2 \cdot 4 = 6 + 10 - 8$

50. **A** $\quad -6(8 + 3) = -6 \cdot 8 + (-6) \cdot 3 = -48 + (-18) = -48 - 18$

Chapter 3 Fractions and Operations

1. **6**   Cuts that give whole numbers of slices for $\frac{2}{3}$ and $\frac{1}{2}$ are 6, 12, 18, etc. 6 is the lowest common denominator AND gives the correct answer.

$$\frac{1}{2} + \frac{2}{3} = \frac{3}{6} + \frac{4}{6} = 1\frac{1}{6}$$

2. **$147.92** $\frac{1}{8} \times \frac{1}{6} = \frac{1}{48}$; $\frac{1}{48} \times \$7100 = \$147.92$

3. **$\frac{11}{25}$** $\frac{44}{100} = \frac{11}{25}$. Numerator and denominator are divided by their greatest common factor, 4.

4. **250 pounds**

$$1000 \times \frac{3}{4} = 750;\ 750 \times \frac{2}{3} = 500;\ 500 \times \frac{1}{2} = 250$$

5. **D** $\frac{1}{3} \div \frac{5}{3} = \frac{1}{3} \times \frac{3}{5} = \frac{1}{5}$

6. **$\frac{1}{2}$**   On Monday she did $\frac{1}{4}$ of the whole backlog. On Tuesday there was $\frac{3}{4}$ of the backlog left. $\frac{3}{4} - \frac{1}{4} = \frac{1}{2}$ of the backlog. Looked at another way, she did $\frac{1}{4} + \frac{1}{4} = \frac{1}{2}$ of the backlog, leaving $\frac{1}{2}$ to be done.

7. **C**   After first reduction, each item costs $\frac{2}{3}$ of the original price. The second reduction leaves $\frac{2}{3}$ of the reduced price, so the final price equals $\frac{2}{3} \times \frac{2}{3} = \frac{4}{9}$ of the original price. The reduction is $\frac{5}{9}$ of the original price.

8. **$6\frac{17}{40}$** $1\frac{5}{8} = 1\frac{25}{40};\ 4\frac{4}{5} = 4\frac{32}{40};$
$$1\frac{25}{40} + 4\frac{32}{40} = 5\frac{57}{40} = 6\frac{17}{40}$$

9. **$28\frac{1}{8}$ pounds**

$$15\frac{3}{4} = 15\frac{6}{8};\ 15\frac{6}{8} + 12\frac{3}{8} = 27\frac{9}{8} = 28\frac{1}{8}$$

10. **$15\frac{13}{20}$ pounds**

$$23\frac{1}{4} = 23\frac{5}{20} = 22\frac{25}{20};\ 7\frac{3}{5} = 7\frac{12}{20};$$
$$22\frac{25}{20} - 7\frac{12}{20} = 15\frac{13}{20}$$

11. **D**   Yes, he did not add 1 when he converted the mixed number to an improper fraction (he multiplied $\frac{3}{4}$ by $\frac{5}{5}$ rather than by $\frac{6}{5}$).

12. **B** $\frac{25}{225} = \frac{5}{45} = \frac{1}{9}$

13. **$2\frac{5}{8}$** $6\frac{1}{2} = 6\frac{4}{8} = 5\frac{12}{8};\ 5\frac{12}{8} - 3\frac{7}{8} = 2\frac{5}{8}$

14. **7 full glasses**

$$7\frac{3}{4} = \frac{31}{4};\ 55 \times \frac{4}{4} = \frac{220}{4};\ \frac{220}{4} \div \frac{31}{4} =$$
$$\frac{220}{4} \times \frac{4}{31} = \frac{220}{31} = 7\frac{3}{31}$$

ANSWERS AND SOLUTIONS

15. $37\frac{9}{16}$ **inches**

$11\frac{9}{16} \times 5 = 55\frac{45}{16}; \frac{1}{8} \times 5 = \frac{5}{8} = \frac{10}{16};$

$55\frac{45}{16} + \frac{10}{16} = 55\frac{55}{16} = 58\frac{7}{16};$

$8 \times 12 = 96; 96 - 58\frac{7}{16} = 37\frac{9}{16}$

16. $\frac{3}{50}$ $\frac{1}{5} = \frac{20}{100} - \frac{14}{100} = \frac{6}{100} = \frac{3}{50}$

17. **1**   by definition

18. $\frac{48}{64}$ $\frac{3}{4} \times \frac{16}{16} = \frac{48}{64}$

19. **C**   Any non-zero number divided by itself is 1.

20. $\frac{2}{3}$ Greatest common factor is 72.

21. $\frac{76}{25}$ $7\frac{3}{5} = \frac{38}{5} \div \frac{5}{2} = \frac{38}{5} \times \frac{2}{5} = \frac{76}{25}$

22. **72**   2 is a whole number so it may be ignored.

       $8 : 2 \times 2 \times 2$
       $24 : 2 \times 2 \times 2 \times 3$
       $36 : 2 \times 2 \times 3 \times 3$

       LCD has the maximum number of each distinct factor: $2 \times 2 \times 2 \times 3 \times 3 = 72$.

23. $\frac{109}{120}$ **gallons**

Common denominator:

$3 : 3$
$5 : 5$
$8 : 2 \times 2 \times 2$

Maximum number of each factor
$2 \times 2 \times 2 \times 3 \times 5 = 120$.

$\frac{1}{3} = \frac{40}{120}; \frac{1}{5} = \frac{24}{120}; \frac{3}{8} = \frac{45}{120};$

$\frac{40}{120} + \frac{24}{120} + \frac{45}{120} = \frac{109}{120}$

24. $46\frac{3}{4}$ $92\frac{10}{20} = 91\frac{30}{20} - 45\frac{15}{20} = 46\frac{15}{20} = 46\frac{3}{4}$

25. $\frac{33}{35}$ $\frac{1}{7} = \frac{10}{70}; \frac{3}{5} = \frac{42}{70}; \frac{2}{10} = \frac{14}{70};$

$\frac{10}{70} + \frac{42}{70} + \frac{14}{70} = \frac{66}{70} = \frac{33}{35}$

26. $\frac{3}{13}$ Overtime pay =

$\$9 \times 1\frac{1}{2} \times 8 = \$9 \times \frac{3}{2} \times 8 = \$108;$

Regular pay = $\$9 \times 40 = \$360;$

Total = $360 + 108 = \$468; \frac{\$108}{\$468} = \frac{3}{13}$

27. **>**   The lower the denominator, the larger the part, so $\frac{3}{54}$ is slightly bigger than $\frac{3}{56}$.

28. **<** $\frac{5}{4} = 1\frac{1}{4} < 1\frac{1}{2}$

29. **>** $\frac{7}{4} > 2; \frac{13}{8} < 2$

30. **=**   Both reduce to $\frac{1}{18}$.

31. $\frac{5}{4}$ $1 = \frac{4}{4}; \frac{4}{4} + \frac{1}{4} = \frac{5}{4}$

32. $\frac{55}{8}$ $6 = \frac{48}{8}; \frac{48}{8} + \frac{7}{8} = \frac{55}{8}$

33. $\frac{127}{10}$ $12 = \frac{120}{10}; \frac{120}{10} + \frac{7}{10} = \frac{127}{10}$

34. $4\frac{1}{4}$ $17 \div 4 = 4\frac{1}{4}$

35. $11\frac{3}{11}$ $124 \div 11 = 11\frac{3}{11}$

36. $1\frac{5}{18}$ $92 \div 72 = 1\frac{20}{72} = 1\frac{5}{18}$

37. **H**

38. **D**

ANSWERS AND SOLUTIONS

39. **G**

40. **I**

41. **E**

42. **Point A** $= -3\frac{3}{4}$

43. **Point C** $= -2\frac{1}{4}$

44. **Point D** $= -\frac{1}{4}$

45. **Point F** $= \frac{3}{4}$

46. **Point G = 2**

47. **4** $64^{\frac{1}{3}} = \sqrt[3]{64} = 4$

48. $\frac{1}{4}$ $16^{-\frac{1}{2}} = \frac{1}{16^{\frac{1}{2}}} = \frac{1}{\sqrt{16}} = \frac{1}{4}$

49. $\frac{1}{9}$ $\left(-\frac{1}{3}\right)^2 = -\frac{1}{3} \times -\frac{1}{3} = \frac{1}{9}$

50. $\frac{8}{125}$ $\left(\frac{2}{5}\right)^3 = \frac{2}{5} \times \frac{2}{5} \times \frac{2}{5} = \frac{8}{125}$

Chapter 4 Decimal Numbers and Operations

1. **>**

2. **<**

3. **=**

4. **<**

5. **>**

6. **C** $\left(-6 \times 10^6\right) \times \left(-2 \times 10^2\right) = 12 \times 10^8 =$
   1.2×10^9

7. **B** $1.235 + (-1.235) = 0$

8. **16.784** $12.389 + 4.3950 = 16.7840 = 16.784$

9. **47.79**

10. **17.1442**

11. **17.85**

12. **8.88**

13. **683.25**

14. **155 miles** $14.00 - 8.37 = 5.63$ gallons

   $5.63 \text{ gallons} \times \dfrac{27.6 \text{ miles}}{\text{gallon}} =$

   155.388 miles

15. **2.5 months**

   $132.50 + 675.00 + 512.50 = 1320$
   $3300 \div 1320 = 2.5$

16. **$149.66** $63.55 \text{ cents} = 0.6355$

   $235,500 \div 1000 = 235.5$

   $0.6355 \times 235.5 = 149.66025$

17. **7.5×10^2 or 750 seconds**

   $\dfrac{2.25 \times 10^8}{3.0 \times 10^5} = 0.75 \times 10^3 = 7.5 \times 10^2$

18. **36.47** $52.7 - 16.23 = 52.70 - 16.23 = 36.47$

19. **6.89** $|-1.45 - (-8.34)| = |-1.45 + 8.34| =$
   $|6.89| = 6.89$

ANSWERS AND SOLUTIONS

20. **4.724** $|2.735 - (-1.989)| = |2.735 + 1.989| = |4.724| = 4.724$

21. **B** The second decimal place to the right of the decimal expresses hundredths.

22. **D** In D, the digit 5 represents units.

23. **$2.53** $0.460 \times \$5.50 = \$2.53$

24. **$9.21** $4 \times \$1.35 = \$5.40$

    $\$5.40 + \$3.29 + \$2.10 = \$10.69$

    $\$20.00 - \$10.69 = \$9.21$

25. **$18.25** $\$0.25 \times 7 = \$1.75$

    $\$20.00 - \$1.75 = \$18.25$

26. **$573.13** $32.75 \times \$17.50 = \$573.125$

27. **$14.25** $\$0.95 \times 15 = \$14.25$

28. **D** $150 \times 6 \times 10^4 = 900 \times 10^4 = 9.0 \times 10^6$

29. **$40.61** $11.74 \times \$3.459 = \$40.608 \approx \$40.61$

30. **B** $\$20.00 \div \$4.599 \approx 4.34877$. But we can't round up because that would cost more than $20.00. So 4.34 is the correct answer.

31. **$278.25** $\$0.265 \times 1050 = \$278.25$.

32. **114.82 square feet**

    $9.45 \times 12.15 = 114.8175$

33. **0.625** $8)\overline{5.000}$ = 0.625

34. **0.06** $50)\overline{3.000}$ = 0.060

35. **0.109375** $64)\overline{7.000000}$ = 0.109375

36. **1.66×10^{-24}**

    $$\frac{1}{6.02 \times 10^{23}} = \frac{10 \times 10^{-1}}{6.02 \times 10^{23}} = 1.66 \times 10^{-24}$$

37. **$1875** $\$0.0125 \times 150{,}000 = \$1875$

38. **$15.45** $8 \times \$10.50 = \$84.00$

    $\$1.17 \times 85 = \$99.45$

    $\$99.45 - \$84.00 = \$15.45$

39. **$13.73** $\$3.98 \times 3.45 = \$13.731 \approx \$13.73$

40. **C** $93{,}000{,}000 = 9.3 \times 10^7$ in scientific notation

41. **D** $1.496 \times 10^9 \times 0.39 = 0.58422 \times 10^9$

42. **47 months**

    $\$19{,}500 \div \$421.55 = 46.26$ months

    She will make her last payment in the 47th month.

43. **$145,390** $1 \div 7.05 \times 10^{-3} \approx 1.418 \times 10^2$

    $1.418 \times 10^2 \times \$1025 \approx \$145{,}390$

44. **47.28** $100 - 52.72 = 100.00 - 52.72 = 47.28$

45. **$558.06** $\$17.50 \times 40 = \$700$

    $\$44.94 + \$10.50 + 7.00 + 79.50 = \$141.94$

    $\$700 - \$141.94 = \$558.06$

46. **358.69 meters**

    $12.35 + 123.56 + 111.23 + 73.4 + 45.65 = 366.19$

    $366.19 - 7.50 = 358.69$

47. **6.0478×10^{24}**

$7.36 \times 10^{22} = 0.0736 \times 10^{24}$

$0.0736 \times 10^{24} + 5.9742 \times 10^{24} = 6.0478 \times 10^{24}$

48. **0.00006022**

49. **6.12 miles** $17.35 - 11.23 = 6.12$ miles

50. **15 trips** $5.7 + 8.6 = 14.3$ miles each way, or 28.6 miles per round trip

13.5 gallons $\times$ 32.5 miles per gallon = 438.75 miles

438.75 miles $\div$ 28.6 miles per trip = 15.34 trips

He would run out of gas on the 16th trip.

Chapter 5 Ratios, Rates, and Proportions

1. **C**   10 feet to 12 feet =

$$\frac{10 \text{ feet}}{12 \text{ feet}} = \frac{10}{12} = \frac{5}{6}$$

2. **$\frac{3}{4}$**   21 students to 28 students =

$$\frac{21 \text{ students}}{28 \text{ students}} = \frac{21}{28} = \frac{3}{4}$$

3. **D**   24 miles to 36 minutes =

$$\frac{24 \text{ miles}}{36 \text{ minutes}} = \frac{2 \text{ miles}}{3 \text{ minutes}}$$

4. **$\frac{5 \text{ leaves}}{2 \text{ twigs}}$**   20 leaves to 8 twigs =

$$\frac{20 \text{ leaves}}{8 \text{ twigs}} = \frac{5 \text{ leaves}}{2 \text{ twigs}}$$

5. **B**   200 miles per 4 hours =

$$\frac{200 \text{ miles}}{4 \text{ hours}} = \frac{50 \text{ miles}}{1 \text{ hour}} = 50\frac{\text{miles}}{\text{hour}}$$

6. **$8.4\frac{\text{ounces}}{\text{mug}}$**   42 ounces for 5 mugs =

$$\frac{42 \text{ ounces}}{5 \text{ mug}} = \frac{8.4 \text{ ounces}}{1 \text{ mug}} =$$

$$8.4\frac{\text{ounces}}{\text{mug}}$$

7. **A**   70 words in 6 sentences =

$$\frac{70 \text{ words}}{6 \text{ sentences}} = \frac{35 \text{ words}}{3 \text{ sentences}} =$$

$$11\frac{2}{3}\frac{\text{words}}{\text{sentence}}$$

8. **$18.75/hour**

$750 for 40 hours = $\dfrac{\$750}{40 \text{ hours}} = \dfrac{\$75}{4 \text{ hours}} =$

$$\frac{\$18.75}{1 \text{ hour}} = \$18.75/\text{hour}$$

9. **$1\frac{1}{2}\frac{\text{model}}{\text{week}}$** $\frac{3}{4}$ of a model in $\frac{1}{2}$ of a week =

$$\frac{\frac{3}{4} \text{ model}}{\frac{1}{2} \text{ week}} =$$

$$\frac{3}{4} \cdot \frac{2 \text{ model}}{1 \text{ week}} = \frac{3}{2} \cdot \frac{1 \text{ model}}{1 \text{ week}} =$$

$$\frac{3 \text{ model}}{2 \text{ week}} = 1\frac{1}{2}\frac{\text{model}}{\text{week}}$$

ANSWERS AND SOLUTIONS

10. **C**

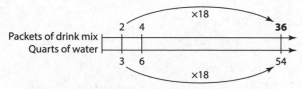

11.

5	6	7	8	9
7.50	9.00	10.50	12.00	13.50

Each hot dog costs $1.50.

12. **B** $\quad \dfrac{7}{12} = \dfrac{x}{28} \rightarrow 28 \cdot \dfrac{7}{12} = 28 \cdot \dfrac{x}{28} \rightarrow$

$\dfrac{28 \cdot 7}{12} = x \rightarrow \dfrac{7 \cdot 7}{3} = x \rightarrow$

$\dfrac{49}{3} = x \rightarrow 16\dfrac{1}{3} = x$

13. **C** $\quad \dfrac{132 \text{ persons}}{40 \text{ square miles}} =$

$\dfrac{132}{40}$ persons per square mile =

3.3 persons per square mile

$40\overline{)132.0}$ ... 3.3

14. **D** $\quad \dfrac{3}{8} = \dfrac{x}{10} \rightarrow 10 \cdot \dfrac{3}{8} = 10 \cdot \dfrac{x}{10} \rightarrow \dfrac{15}{4} =$

$x \rightarrow 3\dfrac{3}{4} = x$

15. **69 miles per hour**

$\dfrac{240 \text{ miles}}{3.5 \text{ hours}} = 68.5 \text{ miles per hour}$

$35\overline{)2400.0}$ ... 68.5

16. **B** $\quad \dfrac{127}{5} = \dfrac{x}{8} \rightarrow 8 \cdot \dfrac{127}{5} = 8 \cdot \dfrac{x}{8} \rightarrow$

$\dfrac{1016}{5} = x \rightarrow 203.2 = x$

17. **A** $\quad \dfrac{20 \text{ g}}{25 \text{ cm}^3} = \dfrac{4}{5} \text{ g/cm}^3 = 0.8 \text{ g/cm}^3$

18. **$1.25 per bottle**

$\dfrac{\$30}{24 \text{ bottles}} = \dfrac{\$5}{4 \text{ bottles}} = \dfrac{\$1.25}{1 \text{ bottle}} =$

$1.25 per bottle

19. **C** $\quad \dfrac{\frac{5}{8} \text{ picture}}{\frac{5}{12} \text{ hour}} = \dfrac{5}{8} \cdot \dfrac{12}{5} \dfrac{\text{picture}}{\text{hour}} =$

$\dfrac{1}{2} \cdot \dfrac{3}{1} \dfrac{\text{picture}}{\text{hour}} = \dfrac{3}{2} \dfrac{\text{picture}}{\text{hour}} = 1\dfrac{1}{2} \text{ pictures/hour}$

20. **D** $\quad \dfrac{35}{2} = \dfrac{x}{14} \rightarrow 14 \cdot \dfrac{35}{2} = 14 \cdot \dfrac{x}{14} \rightarrow$

$7 \cdot 35 = x \rightarrow 245 = x$

21. **D** $\quad \dfrac{6}{1} = \dfrac{x}{3\frac{1}{3}} \rightarrow 3\dfrac{1}{3} \cdot \dfrac{6}{1} = 3\dfrac{1}{3} \cdot \dfrac{x}{3\frac{1}{3}} \rightarrow \dfrac{10}{3} \cdot \dfrac{6}{1} = x$

$\rightarrow 10 \cdot 2 = x \rightarrow 20 = x$

$\dfrac{6}{1} = \dfrac{x}{9\frac{1}{2}} \rightarrow 9\dfrac{1}{2} \cdot \dfrac{6}{1} = 9\dfrac{1}{2} \cdot \dfrac{x}{9\frac{1}{2}} \rightarrow \dfrac{19}{2} \cdot \dfrac{6}{1} = x$

$\rightarrow 19 \cdot 3 = x \rightarrow 57 = x$

22. **B** $\quad \dfrac{9}{16} = \dfrac{x}{96} \rightarrow 96 \cdot \dfrac{9}{16} = 96 \cdot \dfrac{x}{96} \rightarrow 6 \cdot 9 = x$

$\rightarrow 54 = x$

23. **A** $\quad \dfrac{2.5}{20} = \dfrac{x}{90} \rightarrow 90 \cdot \dfrac{2.5}{20} = 90 \cdot \dfrac{x}{90}$

$\rightarrow \dfrac{9 \cdot 2.5}{2} = x \rightarrow 11.25 = x$

24. **D** $\quad \dfrac{3\frac{1}{2}}{4} = \dfrac{x}{10} \rightarrow 10 \cdot \dfrac{3\frac{1}{2}}{4} = 10 \cdot \dfrac{x}{10} \rightarrow \dfrac{5}{2} \cdot \dfrac{7}{2} = x$

$\rightarrow \dfrac{35}{4} = x \rightarrow 8\dfrac{3}{4} = x$

25. **B** $\quad \dfrac{298.9 \text{ miles}}{12.4 \text{ gallons}} = 24.1 \text{ miles per gallon}$

$12.4\overline{)298.9}$ ... 24.1

26. **C** $\dfrac{1}{288} = \dfrac{x}{864} \rightarrow 864 \cdot \dfrac{1}{288} =$

$864 \cdot \dfrac{x}{864} \rightarrow 3 = x$

27. **A** $\dfrac{27}{45} = \dfrac{x}{120} \rightarrow 120 \cdot \dfrac{27}{45} =$

$120 \cdot \dfrac{x}{120} \rightarrow 120 \cdot \dfrac{3}{5} = x \rightarrow$

$\dfrac{24}{1} \cdot \dfrac{3}{1} = x \rightarrow 72 = x$

28. **D** The real-world square is 6 feet.

$\dfrac{1}{5} = \dfrac{x}{6} \rightarrow 6 \cdot \dfrac{1}{5} = 6 \cdot \dfrac{x}{6} \rightarrow \dfrac{6}{5} = x$

$5\overline{)6.0}\,^{1.2}$

29. **B** $\dfrac{3}{2} = \dfrac{x}{8} \rightarrow 8 \cdot \dfrac{3}{2} = 8 \cdot \dfrac{x}{8} \rightarrow$

$4 \cdot 3 = x \rightarrow 12 = x$

30. **C** $\dfrac{12}{\frac{1}{4}} = \dfrac{x}{3\frac{1}{4}} \rightarrow 3\frac{1}{4} \cdot \dfrac{12}{\frac{1}{4}} =$

$3\frac{1}{4} \cdot \dfrac{x}{3\frac{1}{4}} \rightarrow \dfrac{13}{4} \cdot \dfrac{4}{1} \cdot \dfrac{12}{1} = x$

$\rightarrow 13 \cdot 12 = x \rightarrow 156 = x$

156 minutes − 2 hours = 156 minutes − 120 minutes = 36 minutes

$x = 2$ hours 36 minutes

31. **A** $\dfrac{264 \text{ feet}}{1 \text{ min}} = \dfrac{264 \cdot \frac{1}{5280} \text{ mile}}{\frac{1}{60} \text{ hour}} =$

$\dfrac{264}{1} \cdot \dfrac{1}{5280} \cdot \dfrac{60 \text{ mile}}{1 \text{ hour}} =$

$\dfrac{15,840}{5280}$ miles per hour =

3 miles per hour

$5280\overline{)15,840}\,^{3}$

32. **B** $\dfrac{\$3.60}{12 \text{ bars}} = \$0.30$ per bar

$12\overline{)3.60}\,^{0.30}$

33. **C** $\dfrac{99}{4.5} = \dfrac{x}{16} \rightarrow 16 \cdot \dfrac{99}{4.5} = 16 \cdot \dfrac{x}{16} \rightarrow$

$\dfrac{1584}{4.5} = x \rightarrow 352 = x$

34. **Yes** Write $\dfrac{14}{21} = \dfrac{48}{72}$ and cross-multiply:

$14 \cdot 72 = 1008 = 21 \cdot 48$

35. **D** The unit cost of gasoline should be multiplied by the quantity of gasoline to get the total cost.

36. **B** Each crate weighs 40 pounds, so the unit rate is 40 pounds per crate. ($\dfrac{1}{40}$ crates per pound conveys the same relationship, but unit rates are typically concerned with quantity per item, not items per quantity.)

37. **$13.25 per hour**

The unit rate connects the amount of time worked and the amount of pay earned.

38. **$\dfrac{3}{5}$ is the smaller ratio**

Number	3	24
Price	5	40

Number	5	25
Price	8	40

39. **D** $5\overline{)300}\,^{60}$

Dennis's unit rate is $60\dfrac{\text{miles}}{\text{hour}}$.

Multiplying this by time in hours will cancel the hours and leave miles, or distance.

$D = 60t$

40. **No** Write $\dfrac{18}{81} = \dfrac{34}{154}$ and cross-multiply:

$18 \cdot 154 = 2772$, but $81 \cdot 34 = 2754$

41. **Jimmy** $\dfrac{\$48.75}{5 \text{ hours}} = \$9.75/\text{hour}$

$\dfrac{\$58.32}{6 \text{ hours}} = \$9.72/\text{hour}$

42. **\$11.10** $\dfrac{7.77}{12.95} = \dfrac{p}{18.50} \rightarrow 18.50 \cdot \dfrac{7.77}{12.95} =$

$18.50 \cdot \dfrac{p}{18.50} \rightarrow 11.10 = p$

43. **$T = 27n$** $\text{unit price} = \dfrac{\$1620}{60 \text{ baseballs}} =$

$\$27 \text{ per baseball}$

44. **$3\dfrac{2}{3}$ feet** $\dfrac{22}{18} = \dfrac{d}{3} \rightarrow 3 \cdot \dfrac{22}{18} = 3 \cdot \dfrac{d}{3} \rightarrow$

$\dfrac{11}{3} = d \rightarrow 3\dfrac{2}{3} = d$

45. **$1\dfrac{1}{4}$ miles** $\dfrac{75 \text{ miles}}{\text{hour}} \cdot \dfrac{1 \text{ hour}}{60 \text{ minutes}} \cdot \dfrac{1 \text{ minute}}{1} =$

$\dfrac{5 \text{ miles}}{4} = 1\dfrac{1}{4} \text{ miles}$

46. **16 bowls** $\dfrac{20 \text{ bowls}}{5 \text{ quarts}} = \dfrac{n}{9 \text{ quarts}} \rightarrow$

$9 \text{ quarts} \cdot \dfrac{20 \text{ bowls}}{5 \text{ quarts}} =$

$9 \text{ quarts} \cdot \dfrac{n}{9 \text{ quarts}} \rightarrow$

$9 \cdot 4 \text{ bowls} = n \rightarrow 36 \text{ bowls} = n$

$36 \text{ bowls} - 20 \text{ bowls} = 16 \text{ bowls}$

47. **Poplar Hills**

Poplar Hills: $\dfrac{362 \text{ persons}}{0.02 \text{ square mile}} =$

$8{,}100 \text{ persons per square mile}$

San Francisco: $\dfrac{805{,}000 \text{ persons}}{47 \text{ square miles}} =$

$17{,}128 \text{ persons per square mile}$

48. **$D = 24f$** $\dfrac{72}{3} = \dfrac{144}{6} = \dfrac{192}{8} = \dfrac{288}{12}$, the mileage

in miles per gallon

49. **$8\dfrac{1}{3}$ minutes**

$\dfrac{93{,}000{,}000 \text{ miles}}{186{,}000 \frac{\text{miles}}{\text{second}}} =$

$\dfrac{93{,}000 \text{ miles}}{1} \cdot \dfrac{1 \text{ second}}{186 \text{ miles}} = 500 \text{ seconds}$

$\dfrac{500 \text{ seconds}}{1} \cdot \dfrac{1 \text{ minute}}{60 \text{ seconds}} = \dfrac{25}{3} \text{minutes} =$

$8\dfrac{1}{3} \text{ minutes}$

50. **9.7 pounds**

$\dfrac{\$17.37}{\frac{\$1.79}{\text{pound}}} = \dfrac{\$17.37}{1} \cdot \dfrac{1 \text{ pound}}{\$1.79} =$

$\dfrac{17.37}{1.79} \text{ pounds} = 9.7 \text{ pounds}$

Chapter 6 Percents and Applications

1. **17.5%**   2. **80%**   3. **660.5%**

4. **1520%**   5. **0.17%**

Questions 1–5 are solved by multiplying by 100, moving the decimal two places right, and adding the percent sign.

ANSWERS AND SOLUTIONS

6. **60%**   7. **66.67%**   8. **140%**

9. **300%**   10. **287.5%**

Questions 6–10 are solved by converting the fraction into a decimal, moving the decimal two places right, and adding the percent sign.

11. $\frac{13}{40}$ 12. $\frac{3}{5}$ 13. $\frac{3}{50}$

14. $1\frac{17}{20}$ 15. $\frac{7}{2000}$

Questions 11–15 are solved by dividing the percents by 100, clearing decimals by additional multiplications as necessary, and reducing the fractions to lowest terms.

16. **0.11**   17. **0.04**   18. **27.56**

19. **0.071875**   20. **0.000076**

Questions 16–20 are solved by dividing the percents by 100 or moving the decimal point two places to the left.

21. **$19.41** $17.89 \times 1.085 \cong \$19.41$

22. **$143.10** 159.95×0.85 (net from discount) $\times 1.0525$ (sales tax) = $143.10

23. **$26.63** $36.99 \times 0.8 \times 0.9 = \$26.63$

24. **84%** $\frac{168}{1052} = 16\% = $ boxes unloaded by Susan

100% – 16% = 84% = remaining boxes to unload

25. **A**   Either 9250×0.68, or $9250 – ($9250 \times 0.32) = \$6290$.

26. **$1173** $1150 \times 0.06 = \$69$, but the loan is only for $\frac{1}{3}$ of a year, so interest is $\frac{1}{3}$ that, or $23.

$1150 + 23 = \$1173$

27. **$65.95** $1147 \times 0.0575 = \$65.95$

28. **$12,428.57.** $\frac{\$2175}{0.175} = \$12,428.571 \cong \$12,428.57$

29. **15%** $\frac{\$135.20}{1.0625} = \$127.25$, which is the sale price.

$149.70 – $127.25 = \$22.45$ discount

$\frac{\$22.45}{\$149.70} = 14.99\% \cong 15\%$

30. **6 pages**   172 pages $\times 0.285 = 49$ pages of ads. 172×0.25 gives 43 pages as a maximum for 25% ads. The difference is 6 pages.

31. **A** $\frac{2056}{150,000,000} = 0.0000137 =$

$0.00137\% \cong 0.0014\%$

32. **$2400**   This month's sales are 115% of last month's, so $\frac{\$3036}{1.15} = \$2640$. Last month's sales were 110% of the month before, and $\frac{\$2640}{1.10} = \$2400$.

33. **41%** $150,000,000 \times 0.57 = 85,500,000$

$\frac{85,500,000}{207,634,000} = 0.041 = 41\%$

34. **5.6%**   A 6% tax means she must get a price of $\frac{\$10.00}{1.06} = \$9.43$ This is the most she can spend if she uses all $10.00.

$9.99 – $9.43 = \$0.56$

$\frac{0.56}{9.99} \cong 0.056 = 5.6\%$ on the original $9.99 price.

35. **B**   This year's total is 83% of last year's.

$475 \times 0.83 = 394$

36. **43%** $\frac{422,000}{987,000} = 0.4275 \cong 43\%$

37. **20%** $225 – $180 = $45

$$\frac{\$45}{\$225} = 0.20 = 20\%$$

38. **C**   The total, $63.70, is 107.95% of the cost.

$$\frac{\$63.70}{1.0795} = \$59$$

39. **$55.80** $3720 × 0.015 = $55.80

40. **C**   A 15% discount means she pays only 85% of the cost.

$$\frac{\$170.00}{0.85} = \$200$$

41. **C**   Let us say Tom invests $100. He loses 50%, which leaves $50. A 50% increase of $50 is only $25, which raises his investment value to $75—a 25% loss overall.

42. **A**   269 × 1.075 ≅ $289.18, or 269 × 0.075 + $269 ≅ $289.18

43. **+17%**   1,544,400 – 1,320,000 = 224,400 increase.

$$\frac{224,000}{1,320,000} = 0.169 \cong 17\%$$

44. **D** $76 for one month means $76 × 12, or $912, interest per year.

$$\frac{\$912}{\$5000} = 0.1824 \cong 18.2\%$$

45. **A** $$\frac{\$14.49}{0.84} = \$17.25$$

46. **−0.87%**   Suppose Sal invested $100. 100 × 1.10 × 0.95 × 1.02 × 0.93 ≅ 99.13, so Sal lost $0.87, an overall decrease of 0.87%.

47. **$562.67**   6.2% + 1.45% + 14%= 21.65% reduction

100% – 21.65% = 78.35% net take-home

0.7835 × $718.15 ≅ $562.67

48. **D** $555.00 × 0.75 × 0.85 = $353.81

49. **A**   The total weight of a batch is 112 pounds.

$$\frac{9}{112} = 0.080 = 8\%$$

50. **$93,750**   This month is 120% of last month. $\frac{90,000}{1.20} = \$75,000 =$ last month's sales. $75,000 is 80% of the previous month's sales. $\frac{\$75,000}{0.80} = \$93,750 =$ sales two months ago.

Chapter 7 Probability and Statistics

1. **B**   The numbers are roughly proportional, with a proportionality constant of 7.

2. **D** $Y = 7X$

3. **C**   The most probable source of the "noise" in the data is random effects.

4. **B**   A straight line passing through the origin represents a relationship that never needs a constant.

5. **28.5**

6.

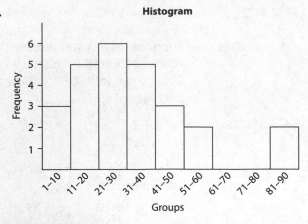

Histogram

Group	1–10	11–20	21–30	31–40	41–50	51–60	61–70	71–80	81–90
Frequency	3	5	6	5	3	2	0	0	2

7. **86, 87**   These data seem fairly far removed from the rest of the data set.

8. **For this distribution, yes.**

9. **12.5%**   The probability of having a boy is $\frac{1}{2}$, independent of the number of boys already born. The probabilities multiply:

$$\frac{1}{2} \times \frac{1}{2} \times \frac{1}{2} = \frac{1}{8} = 0.125 = 12.5\%$$

10. **25%**   The events "having three girls" and "having three boys" are mutually exclusive, so the probabilities for each event are added:

12.5% + 12.5% = 25%

11. **87.5%**   The only way *not* to have a girl is for there to be all boys. Subtract that probability from 1 to get the probability of *at least one* girl:

$$1 - \frac{1}{8} = \frac{7}{8} = 0.875 = 87.5\%$$

12.

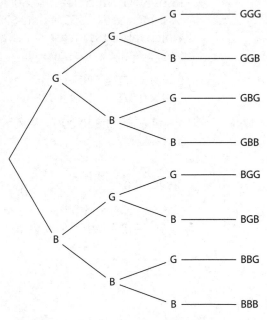

Of the eight possible combinations only three have two girls and one boy: BBB, BBG, BGB, **BGG**, GBB, **GBG**, **GGB**, GGG. Each of the three desired combinations has probability $\frac{1}{8}$, and they are mutually exclusive, so the probabilities are added:

$$\frac{1}{8} + \frac{1}{8} + \frac{1}{8} = \frac{3}{8} = 0.375 = 37.5\%$$

13. Given a fair coin, the most likely result
of six separate flips is three   heads
and three   tails , which is also the mean
and the median of the random data set.

14. **C** The sum of the numbers is 99, and there are 11 numbers.

The mean is $\frac{99}{11} = 9$.

15. **C** The sorted data set is 1, 2, 6, 7, 8, 9, 10, 11, 11, 14, 20.

The median is the number in the middle, 9.

16. **D** 11 appears more than any other number.

17. **D** The highest data value minus the lowest data value = 20 − 1 = 19.

18. $\frac{4}{7}$ There are 20 socks (8 red and 12 black) that, if picked, will *not* make the pair. Picking one of these will require at least a third pick to get a pair. The probability of picking one of those is $\frac{20}{35}$ or $\frac{4}{7}$.

19. $\frac{13}{17}$ Having picked two socks, there are now 34 left in the drawer. The *only way to avoid* making a pair: pick a red sock. The probability of that is $\frac{8}{34}$. Subtracting from 1 gives a probability of $1 - \frac{8}{34} = \frac{26}{34} = \frac{13}{17}$.

20. **D** The next sock must be one of the already drawn three colors. It is impossible to avoid a pair. Impossible events have a zero probability.

21. $\frac{4}{21}$ 4 salespersons out of 21 did this, so the probability is $\frac{4}{21}$.

22. $\frac{10}{21}$ 10 salespeople did that, so the probability is $\frac{10}{21}$.

23. **C** The largest number of people made sales in this range, so that is the mode.

24. $\frac{16}{23}$ We add the probabilities of the two types but must subtract the number of people who fit both categories at the same time to avoid double-counting them.

$$\frac{14}{23} + \frac{13}{23} - \frac{11}{23} = \frac{16}{23}$$

25. $\frac{1}{16}$ The trials are independent and probabilities are multiplied:

$$\frac{1}{2} \times \frac{1}{2} \times \frac{1}{2} \times \frac{1}{2} = \frac{1}{16}$$

26. $\frac{1}{8}$ Of the three-toss combinations that include one head and two tails, only one is in the desired order.

$$\frac{1}{2} \times \frac{1}{2} \times \frac{1}{2} = \frac{1}{8}$$

27. $\frac{1}{27}$ The trials are not run with replacement. There are only 27 numbers left. Picking one specific number leads to the answer.

28. **B** Probabilities are calculated for every terminal event. When that is done, the average gas well has the highest probability.

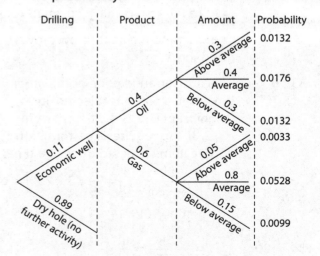

29. **C** Probabilities are calculated for every terminal event. When that is done, the above-average gas well has the lowest probability.

30. **$146.2 million**

    Expected number of producing wells = 11, expected revenue = 11 × $23 million = $253 million; expected number of dry holes = 89, expected cost = 89 × $1.2 million = $106.8 million; profit = revenue – cost = $253 million – $106.8 million = $146.2 million.

31. $\dfrac{63}{64}$ The only way no heads are tossed is if all tails are tossed. That probability is $\dfrac{1}{2} \times \dfrac{1}{2} \times \dfrac{1}{2} \times \dfrac{1}{2} \times \dfrac{1}{2} \times \dfrac{1}{2} = \dfrac{1}{64}$. Since the sum of probabilities equals one, $1 - \dfrac{1}{64} = \dfrac{63}{64}$ is the probability of at least one head.

32. **D** The probability of throwing four tails in a row with a fair coin is $\dfrac{1}{16}$. This is not a rare enough occurrence to support a decision about the fairness of the coin. Since each throw is independent of all others, the probability of throwing another tail with a fair coin is still $\dfrac{1}{2}$, so whatever happens on the next throw proves nothing.

33. **6** Because arrangement, or the order in which a player is selected, is significant (1, 2, 3 is different from 3, 2, 1), this requires a permutation. Three items selected three at a time:

    $_3P_3 = \dfrac{3!}{(3-3)!} = \dfrac{3!}{0!} = \dfrac{3!}{1} = 3 \times 2 \times 1 = 6$.

    Remember: 0! = 1.

34. **120** $_6P_3 = \dfrac{6!}{(6-3)!} = \dfrac{6!}{3!} =$

    $\dfrac{6 \times 5 \times 4 \times 3 \times 2 \times 1}{3 \times 2 \times 1} = 6 \times 5 \times 4 = 120$

35. **252** Here the order of the problems does not matter, so we use a combination.

    $_{10}C_5 = \dfrac{10!}{(10-5)!5!} = \dfrac{10 \times 9 \times 8 \times 7 \times 6}{5 \times 4 \times 3 \times 2 \times 1} =$

    $2 \times 3 \times 2 \times 7 \times 3 = 252$

36. **420** The order in which the instructors sit on a committee does not matter, so we use a combination. Six women selected two at a time = $_6C_2 = \dfrac{6!}{(6-2)!2!} = 15$; eight men selected two at a time = $_8C_2 = \dfrac{8!}{(8-2)!2!} = 28$; 15 × 28 = 420.

37. $\dfrac{3}{7}$ 6 women out of 14 people gives $\dfrac{6}{14} = \dfrac{3}{7}$.

38. **1.45%** $\dfrac{6}{14} \times \dfrac{5}{13} \times \dfrac{4}{12} \times \dfrac{3}{11} = \dfrac{3}{7} \times \dfrac{5}{13} \times \dfrac{1}{3} \times \dfrac{3}{11} = \dfrac{15}{1001} = 0.0145 = 1.45\%$

39. **47.36%** There are 18 winning numbers in the wheel out of 38, so the probability is $\dfrac{18}{38} = 0.4736 = 47.36\%$.

40. $\dfrac{1}{720}$ There are 6! or 720 arrangements. Only one is in alphabetical order. The probability is $\dfrac{1}{720}$.

41.

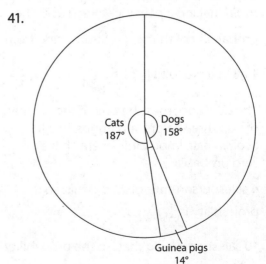

There are 100 items, so each item gets 3.6 degrees.

42. **5040** $_7P_7 = 7! = 5040$

43. $\dfrac{202}{203}$ The only way to avoid a non-Californian is to pick 3 Californians. That works out to

$$\frac{6}{30} \times \frac{5}{29} \times \frac{4}{28} = \frac{1}{5} \times \frac{5}{29} \times \frac{1}{7} =$$

$$\frac{5}{1015} = \frac{1}{203}.$$

Subtracting from 1 gives the probability that the group will have at least one non-Californian: $\dfrac{202}{203}$.

44. **30** The combinations give $5 \times 2 \times 3 = 30$.

45. $\dfrac{5}{98}$ You still have your 5 tickets but now there are only 98 tickets total, so the probability is $\dfrac{5}{98}$.

46. $\dfrac{1}{961}$ There are $31 \times 31 \times 31$ possible combinations but only 31 that have all three digits the same.

$$\frac{31}{31 \times 31 \times 31} = \frac{1}{961}$$

47. **66%** $\text{probability} = \dfrac{\text{number of outcomes}}{\text{number of trials}} =$

$$\frac{165}{250} = 0.66 = 66\%$$

48. **2.70**

Grades	A	B	C	D	F	Total
Credit hours	16	27	18	8	1	**70**
Grade points	4	3	2	1	0	
Total grade points	64	81	36	8	0	**189**

$$\frac{189}{70} = 2.70$$

49. **B** A double grade of 69 gives a weighted average of 80.

50. **D** A double grade of 100 will still leave her short of 90.

Chapter 8 Geometry

1. **1400 square feet**

   Working from the area, the largest plot is 40 feet high. The square is half this height because both plots are 20 feet wide. This makes the dimensions of the triangle 20 feet on each side. The area of a triangle is $\frac{1}{2}bh$.

   The triangle has an area of 200 square feet. (It is also half the area of the small square.) Total area is $800 + 400 + 200$, or 1400 square feet.

2. **A** The major difficulty here is the length of the hypotenuse of the triangle. Each of the triangle's legs is 20 feet, so the hypotenuse is

   $$\sqrt{20^2 + 20^2} = \sqrt{400 + 400} = \sqrt{800} \approx$$

   28.3 feet. Adding the sides gives $20 + 40 + 40 + 20 + 28.3 = 148.3$ feet, but the problem asks for a whole number of feet, which means the answer is 149 feet.

ANSWERS AND SOLUTIONS

3. **It doubles.**

   Doubling the sides a and b gives us

   $\sqrt{(2a)^2 + (2b)^2} = \sqrt{4a^2 + 4b^2} =$

   $\sqrt{4(a^2 + b^2)} = 2\sqrt{a^2 + b^2} = 2c$

4. **C**   For a triangle, $A = \frac{1}{2}bh$. Doubling

   the lengths gives

   $A = \frac{1}{2}(2b)(2h) = \frac{1}{2} \cdot 4bh = 4\left(\frac{1}{2}bh\right)$, or

   four times the area.

5. **5**   Each sphere has a radius $r = 6$
   inches. The surface area is given by
   $4\pi r^2 = 4\pi \cdot 6^2 = 4\pi \cdot 36 = 144\pi \approx$
   $144 \cdot 3.14 = 452.16$. Each sphere has an
   area of 452.16 square inches. Together,
   all three require 1356.48 square inches
   of paint. At 288 square inches a can, this
   means she needs $1356.48 \div 288 = 4.71$
   cans. She must buy 5 whole cans.

6. **B**   A square 4 feet on a side allows a circle of
   radius $r = 2$ feet. The area of this square
   will be $A = \pi r^2 = \pi 2^2 = 4\pi \approx 4 \cdot 3.14 =$
   12.56 square feet.

7. **3.44 square feet**

   The area of the square with a side of length
   $s = 4$ is given by $A = s^2 = 4^2 = 16$ square
   feet. Subtracting the area of the circle gives
   $16 - 12.56 = 3.44$ square feet.

8. **D**   If the area of the circle is equal to the area
   outside the circle, then the area of the
   rectangle is twice the area of the circle.
   The circle, with radius $r = 3$, has an area
   $A = \pi \cdot 3^2 = 9\pi \approx 9 \cdot 3.14 = 28.26$ square
   feet; twice that is 56.52. Dividing this by 6
   gives the result.

9. **C**   Per the formula for the area of a

   trapezoid, $A = \frac{b_1 + b_2}{2}h$, the area of each

   end is 432 square inches. Double this
   and get 864 square inches for the two
   ends. Note that the bottom of the hood
   is open; calculate: The top is 24×36, or
   864 square inches. The back is 16×36,
   or 576 square inches. The sloping front is
   the hypotenuse of a right triangle whose
   legs are 6 and 16 inches. Its length is
   17.1 inches. The area of this piece is then
   17.1×36 or 615.6 square inches. The
   total area is $864 + 864 + 576 + 615.6 =$
   2919.6 square inches.

10. **H**

11. **C**

12. **A**

13. **F**

14. **B**

15. **D**

16. **G**

17. **J**

18. **E**

19. **I**

20. **0.477 cubic centimeters**

   The volume of the cube is $V = s^3 = 1^3 = 1$.

   The sphere, with radius $r = \frac{1}{2}$, has volume

   $V = \frac{4}{3}\pi r^3 = \frac{4}{3}\pi\left(\frac{1}{2}\right)^3 = \frac{4}{3}\pi \cdot \frac{1}{8} = \frac{\pi}{6} \approx$

   $\frac{3.14}{6} = 0.523$. The difference is $1 - 0.523 =$

   0.477 cubic centimeters.

21. **C** The half sphere has the area
$A = \dfrac{4\pi r^2}{2} = 2\pi \cdot 1^2 \approx 2 \cdot 3.14 \cdot 1 =$
6.28. The lateral area of a right cone
is $A = \pi rl$, where l is the slant height.
Use the Pythagorean theorem on a right
triangle with a 1-foot base and a 6-foot
height to find the slant height:
$\sqrt{6^2 + 1^2} = \sqrt{36 + 1} = \sqrt{37} \approx 6.08$. The
lateral area is then $A \approx 3.14 \cdot 1 \cdot 6.08 \approx$
19.1. Adding these two areas yields
25.4 square feet of paintable surface.

22. **44.5 inches**

If one side is x and the other $2x$, the area of the
triangle is
$A = \dfrac{1}{2}bh = \dfrac{1}{2}(x)(2x) = x^2 = 72.25$. Taking
the square root gives $x = 8.5$. The two sides of
the triangle are 8.5 and 17 inches. Using the
Pythagorean theorem, you find that the
hypotenuse is $\sqrt{8.5^2 + 17^2} = \sqrt{72.25 + 289} =$
$\sqrt{361.25} \approx 19$. The perimeter is the sum of the
three numbers: $8.5 + 17 + 19 = 44.5$ inches.

23. **A** A regular hexagon inscribed in a circle
has a side equal in length to the radius
of the circle, since segments drawn from
the center to the vertices of the hexagon
form six equilateral triangles. An apothem
drawn in one of these triangles forms a
right triangle with hypotenuse 3 and half
a side, 1.5, for a base. Use the Pythagorean
theorem to find the apothem:
$\sqrt{3^2 - 1.5^2} = \sqrt{9 - 2.25} = \sqrt{6.75} \approx 2.6$.
The perimeter is $P = 6 \cdot 3 = 18$. The area is
$\dfrac{1}{2}(2.6)(18) = 23.4$ square centimeters.

24. **61.95 square centimeters**

$A = \dfrac{1}{2}aP = \dfrac{1}{2} \cdot 4.13 \cdot 30 = 61.95$

25. **B** The area of the end is 10 square feet
$\left(\dfrac{4 + 6}{2} \cdot 2\right)$. The volume is the area of the
end times the length of the trough:
$10 \cdot 11 = 110$ cubic feet.

26. **6.7 centimeters**

The volume of a right cylinder (a can) is $\left(\pi r^2\right)h$,
the height times the area of one end. With a
3.75-centimeter radius, the area of each
circular end is 44 square centimeters. Dividing
this into 296 cubic centimeters tells us the
height will be 6.7 centimeters high.

27. **B** The circumference of a can
7.5 centimeters in diameter is
$\pi d \approx 3.14 \cdot 7.5 = 23.55$ centimeters.
Adding 1 centimeter for gluing overlap,
this becomes 24.55 centimeters. The
label area is $24.55 \cdot 6.7 = 164.5$ square
centimeters.

28. **64** The volume of a package is $6 \cdot 12 \cdot 3 = 216$
cubic inches. Dividing 13,842 by 216 tells
us that there will be 64 packages per box.

29. **15.75 cubic inches**

The surface area of the box is
$A = 2hl + 2hw + 2lw =$
$2 \cdot 3 \cdot 12 + 2 \cdot 3 \cdot 6 + 2 \cdot 12 \cdot 6 =$
$72 + 36 + 144 = 252$ square inches

The volume of plastic for one box is
$252 \cdot \dfrac{1}{16} = 15.75$ cubic inches per package.

30. **B** Use $C = 2\pi r$ to find the radius of each
ball and $V = \dfrac{4}{3}\pi r^3$ to find each volume.
Dividing the circumference of the soccer
ball by 2π gives a radius of 10.8 and a
volume of 5310. Doing the same for the
basketball gives a radius of 12 and a
volume of 7268 cubic centimeters. The
difference is 1958 cubic centimeters.

31. **150 feet**

    The perimeter of the field is 450 feet. The equilateral triangle has three equal sides, so each will be 150 feet.

32. **2750 square feet**

    The rectangle has an area of 12,500. Use the Pythagorean theorem to find the height of the triangle. The hypotenuse is known, and one leg is half the side of the triangle, so the other leg is $\sqrt{150^2 - 75^2} = \sqrt{22,500 - 5625} = \sqrt{16,875} \approx 130$. The area of the triangle is $\frac{1}{2}bh = \frac{1}{2}(150)(130) = 9750$. The difference is 2750 square feet.

33. **D** If he takes down the fences, the farmer can irrigate a circle 330 feet in radius for an area of 342,119 square feet. If he leaves his fences, he gets four circles with radii of 165 feet. Each small circle has an area of 85,530 square feet, or 342,119 total square feet. There is no difference.

34. **21,716 square feet**

    The square has an area of 15,625 square feet. The semicircle has a radius of 62.5 feet. The area of a circle is $\pi r2$, so an entire circle would have an area of 12,272 feet. However, we need to cover only half that, or 6136 square feet. The sum of 15,625 + 6136 is 21,761 square feet.

35. **10 inches**

    Since the area of the triangle is $\frac{1}{2}bh$, the triangle's other side is 8 inches long. Using the Pythagorean theorem, $a^2 + b^2 = c^2$, we find the hypotenuse, c, to be 10 inches long.

36. **A** The radius of both the cylinder and the half spheres is 6. The volume of the two half spheres is the same as the volume of one whole sphere,
    $$V = \frac{4}{3}\pi r^3 \approx \frac{4}{3} \cdot 3.14 \cdot 6^3 \approx 905.$$
    The volume of the cylinder is
    $$V = \pi r^2 h \approx 3.14 \cdot 6^2 \cdot 50 = 5652.$$ The sum is 6557 cubic feet.

37. **A** The surface area of the side of a cylinder is needed, $A = 2\pi rh \approx 2 \cdot 3.14 \cdot 6 \cdot 50 = 1884$ square feet. The half spheres have the surface area of a whole sphere, $A = 4\pi r^2 \approx 4 \cdot 3.14 \cdot 6^2 \approx 452$ square feet. The sum of the areas is 2336 square feet.

38. **C** The radius is proportional to the cube of the volume, so the volume is proportional to the cube root of the radius. Doubling the volume increases the radius by $\sqrt[3]{2} \approx 1.26$.

39. **262.5 feet**

    A right triangle is formed, with one leg = 250 feet along the ground and the other leg = 85 – 5 feet (the change in height). Using the Pythagorean theorem, we find that the wire is $\sqrt{250^2 + 80^2} = \sqrt{62,500 + 6400} = \sqrt{68,900} \approx 262.5$.

40. **D** The area of the base of the pyramid is 36. The volume is $\frac{1}{3}(36)(20) = 240$. The cone has a circular base with $r = 3$. Its area is $\pi r^2 = \pi(3)^2 \approx 28.27$. The volume of the cone is $V = \frac{1}{3}(28.27)h \approx 9.42h = 240$. Dividing 240 by 9.42 gives the height of the cone, 25.5 feet.

41. **7.1 cubic inches**

    The top is a cone with $r = 1.5$ and h = 6, so $V = \frac{1}{3}\pi r^2 h \approx \frac{1}{3} \cdot 3.14 \cdot 1.5^2 \cdot 6 = 14.13$. Half of that is 7.1.

42. **C** The original box has panels of $7 \cdot 12 = 84$; $9 \cdot 12 = 108$, and $9 \cdot 7 = 63$, which add up to 255 square inches for half the panels. The new box has panels of $3\frac{1}{2} \cdot h$, $4\frac{1}{2} \cdot h$, and $4\frac{1}{2} \cdot 3\frac{1}{2} = 15\frac{3}{4}$ square inches for half the surface area. Adding the new box's dimensions means that $8h + 15\frac{3}{4} = 255$.

    Then, $8h = 239\frac{1}{4}$ square inches, and $h = 29\frac{29}{32}$ inches.

43. **6427 square feet**

The area of the square is 2500. The circles each have $r = 25$, and total area $2\pi r^2 \approx 2 \cdot 3.14 \cdot 25^2 = 3925$ square feet. Total area is 6425 square feet.

44. **314 feet**

The total perimeter is that around two circles with $r = 25$: $2(2\pi r) \approx 2 \cdot 2 \cdot 3.14 \cdot 25 = 314$ feet.

45. **144 inches**

The cube root of the volume is the length of one edge, since $V = l^3$. This gives an edge length of 144 inches.

46. **B** Using the Pythagorean theorem, we find that the length of the other leg is

$\sqrt{11.4^2 - 7^2} = \sqrt{129.96 - 49} = \sqrt{80.96} \approx 9$.

The area of the triangle is $A = \frac{1}{2}bh = \frac{1}{2} \cdot 7 \cdot 9 = 31.5$. The volume of the prism is $V = Bh = 31.5h = 787.5$. Dividing 787.5 by 31.5 gives a height of 25 units.

47. **D** The area of one end is $A = \frac{1}{2}(b_1 + b_2)h =$

$\frac{1}{2} \cdot \left(11 + 7\frac{1}{2}\right) \cdot 3\frac{1}{2} = 32\frac{3}{8}$. Multiplying

by the height of the box gives the

volume: $V = Bh = 32\frac{3}{8} \cdot 7 = 226\frac{5}{8}$ cubic

centimeters.

48. **97.5 square feet**

Using the formula, $A = \frac{\sqrt{3}}{4}s^2 = \frac{\sqrt{3}}{4} \cdot 15^2 =$

$\frac{\sqrt{3}}{4} \cdot 225 \approx \frac{1.732}{4} \cdot 225 \approx 97.4$.

49. **A** Multiplying the given area by 4 and then dividing by $\sqrt{3}$ gives the square of the length of the side: $s^2 = 200$. Take the square root to get the length of a side: $s = \sqrt{200} \approx 14$.

50. **4,676,400 cubic feet**

The volume of the space station is $V = Bh$, where B is the area of the base, which is the same as the area of the hexagonal cross-section. Each side of the hexagon must be 60 feet long. Split the hexagon into six equilateral triangles 60 feet on a side. The area of the

triangle is $A = \frac{\sqrt{3}}{4}s^2 = \frac{\sqrt{3}}{4} \cdot 60^2 =$

$\frac{\sqrt{3}}{4} \cdot 3600 \approx \frac{1.732}{4} \cdot 3600 = 1558.8$.

The hexagon's area is 6 times this: $1558.8 \times 6 = 9352.8$. The volume of the station is $V = Bh = 9352.8 \cdot 500 = 4,676,400$ cubic feet.

Chapter 9 Polynomial and Rational Expressions

1. **C** $2a + 5b - 7 + a - 9b - 6 =$
$2a + 1a + 5b - 9b - 7 - 6 =$
$3a - 4b - 13$

2. **B** $5(3x - 2y + 4) =$
$5 \cdot 3x - 5 \cdot 2y + 5 \cdot 4 =$
$15x - 10y + 20$

3. **A** $(2x + 5) - (5x - 7) =$
$2x + 5 - 5x + 7 =$
$2x - 5x + 5 + 7 =$
$-3x + 12$

4. **5 + 2x**

"five more than twice a number" = "5 more than $2x$" = $5 + 2x$

ANSWERS AND SOLUTIONS

5. **C** 7 and $(y - 1)$ are multiplied, so the expression is a product.

6. $x^3 - 8$

   "eight less than the cube of a number" = "8 less than x^3" = $x^3 - 8$

7. -40 $\frac{9}{5}C + 32 = \frac{9}{5}(-40) + 32 = 9(-8) + 32 =$
   $-72 + 32 = -40$

8. **A** $6x$ and $9y$ are added, so the expression is a sum.

9. **A** The coefficient is the numerical factor in a variable term.

10. **D** Sharon interviews $2s$ households. Seven fewer than $2s$ is $2s - 7$.

11. **B** $(3x^2 + x - 2) + (x^2 - 4x + 7) =$
    $3x^2 + x^2 + x - 4x - 2 + 7 =$
    $4x^2 - 3x + 5$

12. **A** $(3x + 2y) - (2x + 3y) =$
    $3x + 2y - 2x - 3y =$
    $3x - 2x + 2y - 3y = x - y$

13. **C** $(6x^2 + 2x - 4) - (2x^2 - 5x + 1) =$
    $6x^2 + 2x - 4 - 2x^2 + 5x - 1 =$
    $6x^2 - 2x^2 + 2x + 5x - 4 - 1 =$
    $4x^2 + 7x - 5$

14. **A** Add the exponents: $x^3 \cdot x^6 \cdot x^2 =$
    $x^{3+6+2} = x^{11}$

15. **B** $2x^4 \cdot 4x^5 = (2 \cdot 4)x^{4+5} = 8x^9$

16. **D** Subtract exponents: $\dfrac{x^8}{x^2} = x^{8-2} = x^6$

17. **D** $\dfrac{25x^9y^4}{15x^6y^{12}} = \dfrac{5 \cdot 5x^{9-6}}{5 \cdot 3y^{12-4}} = \dfrac{5x^3}{3y^8}$

18. **C** $5x^3y(3xy^2 + 2x^2y^3) =$
    $5x^3y \cdot 3xy^2 + 5x^3y \cdot 3x^2y^3 =$
    $15x^4y^3 + 10x^5y^4$

19. **D** $(3x + 4)(2x - 5) =$
    $3x \cdot 2x - 3x \cdot 5 + 4 \cdot 2x - 4 \cdot 5 =$
    $6x^2 - 15x + 8x - 20 =$
    $6x^2 - 7x - 20$

20. **B** $(x - 2y)(2x - y) =$
    $x \cdot 2x - x \cdot y - 2y$
    $2x^2 - xy - 4xy + 2$
    $2x^2 - 5xy + 2y^2$

21. **C** $\dfrac{12p^3q - 16p^5q^2}{8p^2q^3}$

    $\dfrac{12p^3q}{8p^2q^3} - \dfrac{16p^5q^2}{8p^2q^3}$

    $\dfrac{3p}{2q^2} - \dfrac{2p^3}{q} + \dfrac{5p^2}{4}$

22. **A** $\dfrac{21x^3 - 14x^2}{14x^3 + 21x^2} = \dfrac{7x}{7x}$

23. **A** $\dfrac{9s^3t + 6st^2}{6s^3t + 4st^2} = \dfrac{3st}{2st}$

24. **C** $x + 2 \overline{) 2x^2 + x - 6}$ quotient $2x - 3$

    $\underline{2x^2 + 4x}$
    $-3x -$
    $-3x -$

25. **B** $2x^2 - 4xy - 3y^2 =$
    $2 \cdot 5^2 - 4 \cdot 5(-1) +$
    $2 \cdot 25 + 4 \cdot 5 + 3 \cdot$
    $50 + 20 + 3 = 73$

26. $x^4 - 2x^3 - 7x^2 + 6x + 5$

    Write the highest-deg
    highest, then the next

27. $x^2 + x - 3$

    "the sum of the squar
    less than the number"
    $x - 3$" = $x^2 + x - 3$

28. **C** $-16t^2 + 350 = -1$
    $-16 \cdot 16 + 350 =$

29. **A** The leading coeff
    front of the term

30. **B** $12x^4y + 9x^3y^2 - 6$
    $3x^2y \cdot 4x^2 + 3x^2y \cdot$
    $3x^2y(4x^2 + 3xy -$

21. **C** The half sphere has the area
$A = \dfrac{4\pi r^2}{2} = 2\pi \cdot 1^2 \approx 2 \cdot 3.14 \cdot 1 =$
6.28. The lateral area of a right cone
is $A = \pi r l$, where l is the slant height.
Use the Pythagorean theorem on a right
triangle with a 1-foot base and a 6-foot
height to find the slant height:
$\sqrt{6^2 + 1^2} = \sqrt{36 + 1} = \sqrt{37} \approx 6.08$. The
lateral area is then $A \approx 3.14 \cdot 1 \cdot 6.08 \approx$
19.1. Adding these two areas yields
25.4 square feet of paintable surface.

22. **44.5 inches**

If one side is x and the other $2x$, the area of the
triangle is
$A = \dfrac{1}{2}bh = \dfrac{1}{2}(x)(2x) = x^2 = 72.25$. Taking
the square root gives $x = 8.5$. The two sides of
the triangle are 8.5 and 17 inches. Using the
Pythagorean theorem, you find that the
hypotenuse is $\sqrt{8.5^2 + 17^2} = \sqrt{72.25 + 289} =$
$\sqrt{361.25} \approx 19$. The perimeter is the sum of the
three numbers: $8.5 + 17 + 19 = 44.5$ inches.

23. **A** A regular hexagon inscribed in a circle
has a side equal in length to the radius
of the circle, since segments drawn from
the center to the vertices of the hexagon
form six equilateral triangles. An apothem
drawn in one of these triangles forms a
right triangle with hypotenuse 3 and half
a side, 1.5, for a base. Use the Pythagorean
theorem to find the apothem:
$\sqrt{3^2 - 1.5^2} = \sqrt{9 - 2.25} = \sqrt{6.75} \approx 2.6$.
The perimeter is $P = 6 \cdot 3 = 18$. The area is
$\dfrac{1}{2}(2.6)(18) = 23.4$ square centimeters.

24. **61.95 square centimeters**

$A = \dfrac{1}{2}aP = \dfrac{1}{2} \cdot 4.13 \cdot 30 = 61.95$

25. **B** The area of the end is 10 square feet
$\left(\dfrac{4+6}{2} \cdot 2\right)$. The volume is the area of the
end times the length of the trough:
$10 \cdot 11 = 110$ cubic feet.

26. **6.7 centimeters**

The volume of a right cylinder (a can) is $\left(\pi r^2\right)h$,
the height times the area of one end. With a
3.75-centimeter radius, the area of each
circular end is 44 square centimeters. Dividing
this into 296 cubic centimeters tells us the
height will be 6.7 centimeters high.

27. **B** The circumference of a can
7.5 centimeters in diameter is
$\pi d \approx 3.14 \cdot 7.5 = 23.55$ centimeters.
Adding 1 centimeter for gluing overlap,
this becomes 24.55 centimeters. The
label area is $24.55 \cdot 6.7 = 164.5$ square
centimeters.

28. **64** The volume of a package is $6 \cdot 12 \cdot 3 = 216$
cubic inches. Dividing 13,842 by 216 tells
us that there will be 64 packages per box.

29. **15.75 cubic inches**

The surface area of the box is
$A = 2hl + 2hw + 2lw =$
$2 \cdot 3 \cdot 12 + 2 \cdot 3 \cdot 6 + 2 \cdot 12 \cdot 6 =$
$72 + 36 + 144 = 252$ square inches

The volume of plastic for one box is
$252 \cdot \dfrac{1}{16} = 15.75$ cubic inches per package.

30. **B** Use $C = 2\pi r$ to find the radius of each
ball and $V = \dfrac{4}{3}\pi r^3$ to find each volume.

Dividing the circumference of the soccer
ball by 2π gives a radius of 10.8 and a
volume of 5310. Doing the same for the
basketball gives a radius of 12 and a
volume of 7268 cubic centimeters. The
difference is 1958 cubic centimeters.

31. **150 feet**

    The perimeter of the field is 450 feet. The equilateral triangle has three equal sides, so each will be 150 feet.

32. **2750 square feet**

    The rectangle has an area of 12,500. Use the Pythagorean theorem to find the height of the triangle. The hypotenuse is known, and one leg is half the side of the triangle, so the other leg is $\sqrt{150^2 - 75^2} = \sqrt{22,500 - 5625} = \sqrt{16,875} \approx 130$. The area of the triangle is $\frac{1}{2}bh = \frac{1}{2}(150)(130) = 9750$. The difference is 2750 square feet.

33. **D** If he takes down the fences, the farmer can irrigate a circle 330 feet in radius for an area of 342,119 square feet. If he leaves his fences, he gets four circles with radii of 165 feet. Each small circle has an area of 85,530 square feet, or 342,119 total square feet. There is no difference.

34. **21,716 square feet**

    The square has an area of 15,625 square feet. The semicircle has a radius of 62.5 feet. The area of a circle is $\pi r2$, so an entire circle would have an area of 12,272 feet. However, we need to cover only half that, or 6136 square feet. The sum of 15,625 + 6136 is 21,761 square feet.

35. **10 inches**

    Since the area of the triangle is $\frac{1}{2}bh$, the triangle's other side is 8 inches long. Using the Pythagorean theorem, $a^2 + b^2 = c^2$, we find the hypotenuse, c, to be 10 inches long.

36. **A** The radius of both the cylinder and the half spheres is 6. The volume of the two half spheres is the same as the volume of one whole sphere,
    $$V = \frac{4}{3}\pi r^3 \approx \frac{4}{3} \cdot 3.14 \cdot 6^3 \approx 905.$$
    The volume of the cylinder is
    $V = \pi r^2 h \approx 3.14 \cdot 6^2 \cdot 50 = 5652$. The sum is 6557 cubic feet.

37. **A** The surface area of the side of a cylinder is needed, $A = 2\pi rh \approx 2 \cdot 3.14 \cdot 6 \cdot 50 = 1884$ square feet. The half spheres have the surface area of a whole sphere, $A = 4\pi r^2 \approx 4 \cdot 3.14 \cdot 6^2 \approx 452$ square feet. The sum of the areas is 2336 square feet.

38. **C** The radius is proportional to the cube of the volume, so the volume is proportional to the cube root of the radius. Doubling the volume increases the radius by $\sqrt[3]{2} \approx 1.26$.

39. **262.5 feet**

    A right triangle is formed, with one leg = 250 feet along the ground and the other leg = 85 – 5 feet (the change in height). Using the Pythagorean theorem, we find that the wire is $\sqrt{250^2 + 80^2} = \sqrt{62,500 + 6400} = \sqrt{68,900} \approx 262.5$.

40. **D** The area of the base of the pyramid is 36. The volume is $\frac{1}{3}(36)(20) = 240$. The cone has a circular base with $r = 3$. Its area is $\pi r^2 = \pi(3)^2 \approx 28.27$. The volume of the cone is $V = \frac{1}{3}(28.27)h \approx 9.42h = 240$. Dividing 240 by 9.42 gives the height of the cone, 25.5 feet.

41. **7.1 cubic inches**

    The top is a cone with $r = 1.5$ and $h = 6$, so $V = \frac{1}{3}\pi r^2 h \approx \frac{1}{3} \cdot 3.14 \cdot 1.5^2 \cdot 6 = 14.13$. Half of that is 7.1.

42. **C** The original box has panels of $7 \cdot 12 = 84$; $9 \cdot 12 = 108$, and $9 \cdot 7 = 63$, which add up to 255 square inches for half the panels. The new box has panels of $3\frac{1}{2} \cdot h, 4\frac{1}{2} \cdot h$, and $4\frac{1}{2} \cdot 3\frac{1}{2} = 15\frac{3}{4}$ square inches for half the surface area. Adding the new box's dimensions means that $8h + 15\frac{3}{4} = 255$. Then, $8h = 239\frac{1}{4}$ square inches, and $h = 29\frac{29}{32}$ inches.

43. **6427 square feet**

The area of the square is 2500. The circles each have $r = 25$, and total area $2\pi r^2 \approx 2 \cdot 3.14 \cdot 25^2 = 3925$ square feet. Total area is 6425 square feet.

44. **314 feet**

The total perimeter is that around two circles with $r = 25$: $2(2\pi r) \approx 2 \cdot 2 \cdot 3.14 \cdot 25 = 314$ feet.

45. **144 inches**

The cube root of the volume is the length of one edge, since $V = l^3$. This gives an edge length of 144 inches.

46. **B** Using the Pythagorean theorem, we find that the length of the other leg is $\sqrt{11.4^2 - 7^2} = \sqrt{129.96 - 49} = \sqrt{80.96} \approx 9$. The area of the triangle is $A = \frac{1}{2}bh = \frac{1}{2} \cdot 7 \cdot 9 = 31.5$. The volume of the prism is $V = Bh = 31.5h = 787.5$. Dividing 787.5 by 31.5 gives a height of 25 units.

47. **D** The area of one end is $A = \frac{1}{2}(b_1 + b_2)h = \frac{1}{2} \cdot \left(11 + 7\frac{1}{2}\right) \cdot 3\frac{1}{2} = 32\frac{3}{8}$. Multiplying by the height of the box gives the volume: $V = Bh = 32\frac{3}{8} \cdot 7 = 226\frac{5}{8}$ cubic centimeters.

48. **97.5 square feet**

Using the formula, $A = \frac{\sqrt{3}}{4}s^2 = \frac{\sqrt{3}}{4} \cdot 15^2 = \frac{\sqrt{3}}{4} \cdot 225 \approx \frac{1.732}{4} \cdot 225 \approx 97.4$.

49. **A** Multiplying the given area by 4 and then dividing by $\sqrt{3}$ gives the square of the length of the side: $s^2 = 200$. Take the square root to get the length of a side: $s = \sqrt{200} \approx 14$.

50. **4,676,400 cubic feet**

The volume of the space station is $V = Bh$, where B is the area of the base, which is the same as the area of the hexagonal cross-section. Each side of the hexagon must be 60 feet long. Split the hexagon into six equilateral triangles 60 feet on a side. The area of the triangle is $A = \frac{\sqrt{3}}{4}s^2 = \frac{\sqrt{3}}{4} \cdot 60^2 = \frac{\sqrt{3}}{4} \cdot 3600 \approx \frac{1.732}{4} \cdot 3600 = 1558.8$. The hexagon's area is 6 times this: $1558.8 \times 6 = 9352.8$. The volume of the station is $V = Bh = 9352.8 \cdot 500 = 4,676,400$ cubic feet.

Chapter 9 Polynomial and Rational Expressions

1. **C** $2a + 5b - 7 + a - 9b - 6 =$
   $2a + 1a + 5b - 9b - 7 - 6 =$
   $3a - 4b - 13$

2. **B** $5(3x - 2y + 4) =$
   $5 \cdot 3x - 5 \cdot 2y + 5 \cdot 4 =$
   $15x - 10y + 20$

3. **A** $(2x + 5) - (5x - 7) =$
   $2x + 5 - 5x + 7 =$
   $2x - 5x + 5 + 7 =$
   $-3x + 12$

4. **5 + 2x**

   "five more than twice a number" = "5 more than $2x$" = $5 + 2x$

5. **C**   7 and $(y - 1)$ are multiplied, so the expression is a product.

6. $x^3 - 8$

   "eight less than the cube of a number" = "8 less than x^3" = $x^3 - 8$

7. -40 $\frac{9}{5}C + 32 = \frac{9}{5}(-40) + 32 = 9(-8) + 32 =$
   $-72 + 32 = -40$

8. **A** $6x$ and $9y$ are added, so the expression is a sum.

9. **A**   The coefficient is the numerical factor in a variable term.

10. **D**   Sharon interviews $2s$ households. Seven fewer than $2s$ is $2s - 7$.

11. **B** $(3x^2 + x - 2) + (x^2 - 4x + 7) =$
    $3x^2 + x^2 + x - 4x - 2 + 7 =$
    $4x^2 - 3x + 5$

12. **A** $(3x + 2y) - (2x + 3y) =$
    $3x + 2y - 2x - 3y =$
    $3x - 2x + 2y - 3y = x - y$

13. **C** $(6x^2 + 2x - 4) - (2x^2 - 5x + 1) =$
    $6x^2 + 2x - 4 - 2x^2 + 5x - 1 =$
    $6x^2 - 2x^2 + 2x + 5x - 4 - 1 =$
    $4x^2 + 7x - 5$

14. **A**   Add the exponents: $x^3 \cdot x^6 \cdot x^2 =$
    $x^{3+6+2} = x^{11}$

15. **B** $2x^4 \cdot 4x^5 = (2 \cdot 4)x^{4+5} = 8x^9$

16. **D**   Subtract exponents: $\frac{x^8}{x^2} = x^{8-2} = x^6$

17. **D** $\frac{25x^9y^4}{15x^6y^{12}} = \frac{5 \cdot 5x^{9-6}}{5 \cdot 3y^{12-4}} = \frac{5x^3}{3y^8}$

18. **C** $5x^3y(3xy^2 + 2x^2y^3) =$
    $5x^3y \cdot 3xy^2 + 5x^3y \cdot 3x^2y^3 =$
    $15x^4y^3 + 10x^5y^4$

19. **D** $(3x + 4)(2x - 5) =$
    $3x \cdot 2x - 3x \cdot 5 + 4 \cdot 2x - 4 \cdot 5 =$
    $6x^2 - 15x + 8x - 20 =$
    $6x^2 - 7x - 20$

20. **B** $(x - 2y)(2x - y) =$
    $x \cdot 2x - x \cdot y - 2y \cdot 2x + 2y \cdot y =$
    $2x^2 - xy - 4xy + 2y^2 =$
    $2x^2 - 5xy + 2y^2$

21. **C** $\frac{12p^3q - 16p^5q^2 + 10p^4q^4}{8p^2q^3} =$
    $\frac{12p^3q}{8p^2q^3} - \frac{16p^5q^2}{8p^2q^3} + \frac{10p^4q^4}{8p^2q^3} =$
    $\frac{3p}{2q^2} - \frac{2p^3}{q} + \frac{5p^2q}{4}$

22. **A** $\frac{21x^3 - 14x^2}{14x^3 + 21x^2} = \frac{7x^2(3x - 2)}{7x^2(2x + 3)} = \frac{3x - 2}{2x + 3}$

23. **A** $\frac{9s^3t + 6st^2}{6s^3t + 4st^2} = \frac{3st(3s^2 + 2t)}{2st(3s^2 + 2t)} = \frac{3}{2}$

24. **C**
$$\begin{array}{r} 2x - 3 \\ x + 2 \overline{)\,2x^2 + x - 6} \\ \underline{2x^2 + 4x} \\ -3x - 6 \\ \underline{-3x - 6} \end{array}$$

25. **B** $2x^2 - 4xy - 3y^2 =$
    $2 \cdot 5^2 - 4 \cdot 5(-1) + 3(-1)^2 =$
    $2 \cdot 25 + 4 \cdot 5 + 3 \cdot 1 =$
    $50 + 20 + 3 = 73$

26. $x^4 - 2x^3 - 7x^2 + 6x + 5$

   Write the highest-degree term, then the next highest, then the next, etc.

27. $x^2 + x - 3$

   "the sum of the square of a number and three less than the number" = "the sum of x^2 and $x - 3$" = $x^2 + x - 3$

28. **C** $-16t^2 + 350 = -16 \cdot 4^2 + 350 =$
    $-16 \cdot 16 + 350 = -256 + 350 = 94$ feet

29. **A**   The leading coefficient is the number in front of the term with the largest exponent.

30. **B** $12x^4y + 9x^3y^2 - 6x^2y^2 =$
    $3x^2y \cdot 4x^2 + 3x^2y \cdot 3xy - 3x^2y \cdot 2y =$
    $3x^2y(4x^2 + 3xy - 2y)$

ANSWERS AND SOLUTIONS

31. D $\quad 3x^2 - 8x + 4 =$
$3x^2 - 6x - 2x + 4 =$
$3x(x - 2) - 2(x - 2) =$
$(x - 2)(3x - 2)$

32. C $\quad 2x^2 - xy - y^2 =$
$2x^2 - 2xy + xy - y^2 =$
$2x(x - y) + y(x - y) =$
$(x - y)(2x + y)$

33. A $\quad 12x^2y + 40xy - 32y =$
$4y[3x^2 + 10x - 8] =$
$4y[3x^2 - 2x + 12x - 8] =$
$4y[x(3x - 2) + 4(3x - 2)] =$
$4y(3x - 2)(x + 4)$

34. $(4x - 9y)(4x + 9y)$

$16x^2 - 81y^2 = (4x)^2 - (9y)^2 = (4x - 9y)(4x + 9y)$

35. $2x^2 = x + 5$

"twice the square of a number is five more than the number" → "twice the square of a number = five more than the number" → "twice x^2 = five more than x" → $2x^2 = x + 5$

36. A The degree of a polynomial in a single variable is the largest exponent.

37. D $\quad \dfrac{d}{t + 4} = \dfrac{390}{2 + 4} = \dfrac{390}{6} = 65$ miles per hour

38. C $\quad \dfrac{2}{3x^2} + \dfrac{5}{6x} =$

$\dfrac{2}{2} \cdot \dfrac{2}{3x^2} + \dfrac{x}{x} \cdot \dfrac{5}{6x} =$

$\dfrac{4}{6x^2} + \dfrac{5x}{6x^2} = \dfrac{4 + 5x}{6x^2}$

39. B $\quad \dfrac{2x - 5}{5x + 10} + \dfrac{x + 1}{3x + 6} =$

$\dfrac{2x - 5}{5(x + 2)} + \dfrac{x + 1}{3(x + 2)} =$

$\dfrac{3}{3} \cdot \dfrac{2x - 5}{5(x + 2)} + \dfrac{5}{5} \cdot \dfrac{x + 1}{3(x + 2)} =$

$\dfrac{6x - 15}{15(x + 2)} + \dfrac{5x + 5}{15(x + 2)} = \dfrac{11x - 10}{15(x + 2)}$

40. D $\quad \dfrac{3x}{10y} - \dfrac{4y}{15x} =$

$\dfrac{3x}{3x} \cdot \dfrac{3x}{10y} - \dfrac{2y}{2y} \cdot \dfrac{4y}{15x} =$

$\dfrac{9x^2}{30xy} - \dfrac{8y^2}{30xy} = \dfrac{9x^2 - 8y^2}{30xy}$

41. D $\quad \dfrac{3x}{2x - 10} - \dfrac{x}{2x + 6} =$

$\dfrac{3x}{2(x - 5)} - \dfrac{x}{2(x + 3)} =$

$\dfrac{x + 3}{x + 3} \cdot \dfrac{3x}{2(x - 5)} - \dfrac{x - 5}{x - 5} \cdot \dfrac{x}{2(x + 3)} =$

$\dfrac{3x^2 + 9x}{2(x - 5)(x + 3)} - \dfrac{x^2 - 5x}{2(x - 5)(x + 3)} =$

$\dfrac{3x^2 + 9x - x^2 + 5x}{2(x - 5)(x + 3)} =$

$\dfrac{2x^2 + 14x}{2(x - 5)(x + 3)} =$

$\dfrac{2x(x + 7)}{2(x - 5)(x + 3)} =$

$\dfrac{x(x + 7)}{(x - 5)(x + 3)}$

42. C $\quad \dfrac{x + 1}{2x - 4} + \dfrac{x - 1}{2x + 4} - \dfrac{2x}{x^2 - 4} =$

$\dfrac{x + 1}{2(x - 2)} + \dfrac{x - 1}{2(x + 2)} - \dfrac{2x}{(x - 2)(x + 2)} =$

$\dfrac{x + 2}{x + 2} \cdot \dfrac{x + 1}{2(x - 2)} + \dfrac{x - 2}{x - 2} \cdot \dfrac{x - 1}{2(x + 2)} -$

$\dfrac{2}{2} \cdot \dfrac{2x}{(x - 2)(x + 2)} = \dfrac{x^2 + 3x + 2}{2(x - 2)(x + 2)} +$

$\dfrac{x^2 - 3x + 2}{2(x - 2)(x + 2)} - \dfrac{4x}{2(x - 2)(x + 2)} =$

$\dfrac{2x^2 - 4x + 4}{2(x - 2)(x + 2)} = \dfrac{2(x^2 - 2x + 2)}{2(x - 2)(x + 2)} =$

$\dfrac{x^2 - 2x + 2}{(x - 2)(x + 2)}$

43. A $\dfrac{3ax^4}{8b^3y} \cdot \dfrac{6b^3x^5}{9a^6y^3} =$

$\dfrac{x^4}{4y} \cdot \dfrac{x^5}{a^5y^3} =$

$\dfrac{x^4x^5}{4a^5yy^3} = \dfrac{x^9}{4a^5y^4}$

44. B $\dfrac{x^2 - 2x - 3}{x^2 + 3x} \cdot \dfrac{x^2 - 9}{x^2 + 2x + 1} =$

$\dfrac{(x-3)(x+1)}{x(x+3)} \cdot \dfrac{(x-3)(x+3)}{(x+1)(x+1)} =$

$\dfrac{x-3}{x} \cdot \dfrac{x-3}{x+1} =$

$\dfrac{(x-3)^2}{x(x+1)}$

45. D $\dfrac{20x^2y^5}{27a^6b} \div \dfrac{10b^2x^6}{9a^8y^3} =$

$\dfrac{20x^2y^5}{27a^6b} \cdot \dfrac{9a^8y^3}{10b^2x^6} =$

$\dfrac{2y^5}{3b} \cdot \dfrac{a^2y^3}{b^2x^4} = \dfrac{2a^2y^8}{3b^3x^4}$

46. A $\dfrac{4x+8}{x^2+3x} \div \dfrac{x^2-4}{x^2+x-6} =$

$\dfrac{4x+8}{x^2+3x} \cdot \dfrac{x^2+x-6}{x^2-4} =$

$\dfrac{4(x+2)}{x(x+3)} \cdot \dfrac{(x+3)(x-2)}{(x+2)(x-2)} =$

$\dfrac{4}{x} \cdot \dfrac{1}{1} = \dfrac{4}{x}$

47. D $\dfrac{x^2-5x}{4x^2} \cdot \dfrac{x^2-7x+12}{x^2-16} \div \dfrac{2x-10}{x^2+2x-8} =$

$\dfrac{x^2-5x}{4x^2} \cdot \dfrac{x^2-7x+12}{x^2-16} \cdot \dfrac{x^2+2x-8}{2x-10} =$

$\dfrac{x(x-5)}{4x^2} \cdot \dfrac{(x-3)(x-4)}{(x-4)(x+4)} \cdot \dfrac{(x-2)(x+4)}{2(x-5)} =$

$\dfrac{1}{4x} \cdot \dfrac{x-3}{1} \cdot \dfrac{x-2}{2} =$

$\dfrac{(x-3)(x-2)}{8x}$

48. C $\dfrac{3x^2+7x-2}{2x^2-7x+3} =$

$\dfrac{3(-4)^2+7(-4)-2}{2(-4)^2-7(-4)+3} =$

$\dfrac{3 \cdot 16 + 7(-4) - 2}{2 \cdot 16 - 7(-4) + 3} =$

$\dfrac{48 - 28 - 2}{32 + 28 + 3} =$

$\dfrac{18}{63} = \dfrac{2}{7}$

49. $\dfrac{x+5}{x-5}$

"the quotient of 5 more than a number and 5 less than the number" = "the quotient of $x+5$ and $x-5$" $= \dfrac{x+5}{x-5}$

50. $\dfrac{p-1000}{3}$

After the donation to charity, there are $p - 1000$ dollars left. This is split evenly between three people, so each person gets $\dfrac{p-1000}{3}$ dollars.

Chapter 10 Solving Equations and Inequalities

1. **$p = 17$** $p - 5 + 5 = 12 + 5 \rightarrow p + 0 = 17$
   $\rightarrow p = 17$

2. **$s = -8$** $\dfrac{7s}{7} = \dfrac{-56}{7} \rightarrow \dfrac{1s}{1} = -8 \rightarrow s = -8$

3. **$x = 4$** $-3x + 17 = 5 \rightarrow$
   $-3x + 17 - 17 = 5 - 17 \rightarrow$
   $-3x = -12 \rightarrow$
   $\dfrac{-3x}{-3} = \dfrac{-12}{-3} \rightarrow x = 4$

4. **$a = 1$** $\dfrac{6(a - 8)}{6} = \dfrac{-42}{6} \rightarrow a - 8 = -7$
   $\rightarrow a - 8 + 8 = -7 + 8 \rightarrow a = 1$

5. **no solution** $5x + 2(x - 9) = 7x + 10 \rightarrow$
   $5x + 2x - 18 = 7x + 10 \rightarrow$
   $7x - 18 = 7x + 10 \rightarrow$
   $7x - 18 - 7x =$
   $7x + 10 - 7x \; -18 = 10.$ This
   equation is true for no value of x.

6. **24** $7(b + 11) = 245 \rightarrow$
   $\dfrac{7(b + 11)}{7} = \dfrac{245}{7} \rightarrow$
   $b + 11 = 35 \rightarrow$
   $b + 11 - 11 = 35 - 11 \rightarrow b = 24$

7. **35** $95 = \dfrac{9}{5}C + 32 \rightarrow$
   $95 - 32 = \dfrac{9}{5}C + 32 - 32 \rightarrow$
   $63 = \dfrac{9}{5}C \rightarrow$
   $\dfrac{5}{9} \cdot 63 = \dfrac{5}{9} \cdot \dfrac{9}{5}C \rightarrow$
   $5 \cdot 7 = C \rightarrow C = 35$

8. **$x > \dfrac{y - b}{m}$** $y - b < mx + b - b \rightarrow$
   $y - b < mx \rightarrow$
   $\dfrac{y - b}{m} < \dfrac{mx}{m} \rightarrow \dfrac{y - b}{m} < x$

9. **5:00 p.m.** $5c + 15 = 40 \rightarrow$
   $5c + 15 - 15 = 40 - 15 \rightarrow$
   $5c = 25 \rightarrow$
   $\dfrac{5c}{5} = \dfrac{25}{5} \rightarrow$
   $c = 5$ hours after noon

10. **25 centimeters**
    $2(w + 5) + 2w = 90 \rightarrow$
    $2w + 10 + 2w = 90 \rightarrow$
    $4w + 10 = 90 \rightarrow$
    $4w + 10 - 10 = 90 - 10 \rightarrow$
    $4w = 80 \rightarrow$
    $\dfrac{4w}{4} = \dfrac{80}{4} \rightarrow$
    $w = 20$
    $l = 20 + 5 = 25$

11. **B** Total cost of m bags of milo =
    $50m$; total cost of s bags of
    soybean = $40s$; total seed cost =
    $50m + 40s = 2000$.

12. **5 seconds** When the rock strikes the
    ground, $h = 0$;
    $80t - 16t^2 = 0 \rightarrow$
    $16t(5 - t) = 0 \rightarrow$
    $16t = 0$ or $5 - t = 0 \rightarrow$
    $\dfrac{16t}{16} = \dfrac{0}{16}$ or $5 - t + t =$
    $0 + t \rightarrow t = 0$ or $t = 5$

13. **$k \geq 8$**

$3k - 7 + 7 \geq 17 + 7 \rightarrow 3k \geq 24 \rightarrow$
$\dfrac{3k}{3} \geq \dfrac{24}{3} \rightarrow k \geq 8$

14. **C**

$-2x - 3 + 3 < 3 + 3 \rightarrow -2x < 6$
$\rightarrow \dfrac{-2x}{-2} > \dfrac{6}{-2} \rightarrow x > -3$

15. **A**

Time for 1ˢᵗ train: t; distance: $120t$.
Time for 2ⁿᵈ train: $t - 2$; distance: $80(t - 2)$.

16. **(2, –1)**

$3x + y = 5 \rightarrow$
$3x + y - 3x = 5 - 3x \rightarrow$
$y = 5 - 3x$

$2x - 3y = 7 \rightarrow$
$2x - 3(5 - 3x) = 7 \rightarrow$
$2x - 15 + 9x = 7 \rightarrow$
$11x - 15 = 7 \rightarrow$
$11x - 15 + 15 = 7 + 15 \rightarrow$
$11x = 22 \rightarrow$
$\dfrac{11x}{11} = \dfrac{22}{11} \rightarrow x = 2$

$y = 5 - 3x \rightarrow$
$y = 5 - 3 \cdot 2 \rightarrow$
$y = 5 - 6 \rightarrow$
$y = -1$

17. **D**

With r milliliters of solution added to the cylinder each minute, after 60 minutes $60r$ milliliters will be added to the 72 milliliters already in the cylinder. The total amount $60r + 72$ cannot exceed the capacity of the cylinder, so it must be ≤ 500.

18. **$x = -\dfrac{5}{7}$**

$4x - 2(3x + 7) = 6 + 5(x - 3) \rightarrow$
$4x - 6x - 14 = 6 + 5x - 15 \rightarrow$
$-2x - 14 = 5x - 9 \rightarrow$
$-2x - 14 - 5x = 5x - 9 - 5x \rightarrow$
$-7x - 14 = -9 \rightarrow$
$-7x - 14 + 14 = -9 + 14 \rightarrow$
$-7x = 5 \rightarrow \dfrac{-7x}{-7} = \dfrac{5}{-7} \rightarrow$
$x = -\dfrac{5}{7}$

19. **4 years**

In y year, Janie will grow $2\frac{1}{2}y$, or $\dfrac{5}{2}y$, inches. $\dfrac{5}{2}y + 38 \geq 48 \rightarrow$
$\dfrac{5}{2}y + 38 - 38 \geq 48 - 38 \rightarrow$
$\dfrac{5}{2}y \geq 10 \rightarrow \dfrac{2}{5} \cdot \dfrac{5}{2}y \geq \dfrac{2}{5} \cdot \dfrac{10}{1} \rightarrow$
$y \geq 2 \cdot 2 \rightarrow y \geq 4$

20. **4 pounds**

p pounds of peanuts have a total value of $2p$ dollars.
c pounds of cashews have a total value of $7c$ dollars.
10 pounds of mixture has a total value of $5 \cdot 10 = 50$ dollars.

$2p + 7c = 50$; also, $p + c = 10$
$p + c = 10 \rightarrow p + c - p = 10 - p \rightarrow$
$c = 10 - p$
$2p + 7c = 50 \rightarrow$
$2p + 7(10 - p) = 50 \rightarrow$
$2p + 70 - 7p = 50 \rightarrow$
$-5p + 70 = 50 \rightarrow$
$-5p + 70 - 70 = 50 - 70 \rightarrow$
$-5p = -20 \rightarrow$
$\dfrac{-5p}{-5} = \dfrac{-20}{-5} \rightarrow p = 4$

21. **all values of x**

$3x - 2(x - 1) = 2(x + 1) - x \rightarrow$
$3x - 2x + 2 = 2x + 2 - x \rightarrow$
$x + 2 = x + 2 \rightarrow x + 2 - x =$
$x + 2 - x \rightarrow 2 = 2$, which is true for all x.

22. **D**

17 red blocks weigh $17r$ ounces; 13 blue blocks weigh $13b$ ounces. Total weight is $17r + 13b = 99$.

23. **$r > 0$**

The weight of any object must be a positive number.

24. **7.5 quarts** The amount of pure antifreeze is the concentration times the amount of solution. Starting with $0.50 \cdot 5$ quarts of pure antifreeze and ending with $0.20(5 + w)$ quarts of pure antifreeze, $0.50 \cdot 5 = 0.20(5 + w)$, since the amount of pure antifreeze remains constant.

$$0.50 \cdot 5 = 0.20(5 + w) \to$$
$$2.5 = 1 + 0.2w \to$$
$$2.5 - 1 = 1 + 0.2w - 1 \to$$
$$1.5 = 0.2w \to \frac{1.5}{0.2} = \frac{0.2w}{0.2} \to$$
$$7.5 = w$$

25. **B** The area of the base is given by $B = lw = 6w$; the perimeter of the base is given by $p = 2l + 2w = 2 \cdot 6 + 2w = 12 + 2w$. The surface area is given by $SA = ph + 2B = (12 + 2w)h + 2 \cdot 6w = 12h + 2hw + 12w = 12h + 12w + 2hw = 86 \cdot$

26. $x = -2$ or $x = 12$

$$x^2 - 10x - 24 = 0 \to$$
$$(x + 2)(x - 12) = 0$$
$$x + 2 = 0 \text{ or } x - 12 = 0$$
$$x = -2 \text{ or } x = 12$$

27. **(–3, –2)**

$$\begin{array}{l} 3 \cdot \\ 5 \cdot \end{array} \begin{cases} 6x - 5y = -8 \\ 4x + 3y = -18 \end{cases} \to$$

$$\begin{cases} 18x - 15y = -24 \\ 20x + 15y = -90 \end{cases} \to$$

$$38x = -114 \to \frac{38x}{38} = \frac{-114}{38} \to$$
$$x = -3 \to 4x + 3y = -18 \to$$
$$4(-3) + 3y = -18 \to$$
$$-12 + 3y = -18 \to$$
$$-12 + 3y + 12 = -18 + 12 \to$$
$$3y = -6 \to$$
$$\frac{3y}{3} = \frac{-6}{3} \to y = -2$$

28. **C** Shading to the right of –2 indicates sense of "greater than" and the open endpoint indicates "strict" inequality.

29. $x < 8$

$$2x - 4x + 9 > 4x - 7 - 4x \to$$
$$-2x + 9 > -7 \to$$
$$-2x + 9 - 9 > -7 - 9 \to$$
$$-2x > -16 \to$$
$$\frac{-2x}{-2} < \frac{-16}{-2} \to x < 8$$

30. **no solution**

$$2 \cdot \begin{cases} 3x - 5y = 2 \\ -6x + 10y = 7 \end{cases} \to$$

$$\begin{cases} 6x - 10y = 4 \\ -6x + 10y = 7 \end{cases} \to 0 = 11$$

31. **B** At \$40 per lawn, mowing x lawns will bring in \$40x. This is added to the \$420 already saved. The total cannot be smaller than \$1500, so a "greater than" inequality is used.

32. $x = \dfrac{7 \pm \sqrt{17}}{4}$

$2x^2 - 7x + 4 = 0$ cannot be factored; use the quadratic formula $x = \dfrac{-b \pm \sqrt{b^2 - 4ac}}{2a}$, with $a = 2, b = -7$, and $c = 4$:

$$x = \frac{-(-7) \pm \sqrt{(-7)^2 - 4 \cdot 2 \cdot 4}}{2 \cdot 2} =$$
$$\frac{7 \pm \sqrt{49 - 32}}{4} = \frac{7 \pm \sqrt{17}}{4}$$

33. **8 centimeters**

For a square, $A = s^2$, so
$$64 = s^2 \to \pm\sqrt{64} = \sqrt{s^2} \to \pm 8 = s.$$

Lengths are positive, so the negative solution is discarded.

ANSWERS AND SOLUTIONS

34. A $\quad -\dfrac{2}{3}x \ge 4 \to$

$$-\dfrac{3}{2}\left(-\dfrac{2}{3}x\right) \le -\dfrac{3}{2}\cdot 4 \to x \le -6$$

35. $x = \pm 5$ $\quad \sqrt{x^2} = \pm\sqrt{25} \to x = \pm 5$

36. width is 5 units, length is 9 units

$A = lw = 45;\ l = w + 4$
$(w + 4)w = 45 \to$
$w^2 + 4w - 45 = 0 \to (w + 9)(w - 5) = 0$
$w + 9 = 0$ or $w - 5 = 0 \to w = -9$ or $w = 5$,
but width cannot be negative, so $w = 5$,
$l = w + 4 = 5 + 4 = 9$.

37. 28 gallons of the strong detergent, 32 gallons of the weak

The amount of pure detergent in a solution is the concentration times the amount of solution. There are 0.90s gallons of pure detergent in s gallons of the strong solution, and 0.15w gallons of pure detergent in w gallons of the weak solution. These are added together to get $0.50 \cdot 60 = 30$ gallons of pure detergent in the mild solution: $0.90s + 0.15w = 30$. Also, $s + w = 60$.
$s + w = 60 \to s + w - s = 60 - s \to w = 60 - s$
$0.90s + 0.15w = 30 \to$
$0.90s + 0.15(60 - s) = 30 \to$
$0.90s + 9 - 0.15s = 30 \to 0.75s + 9 = 30 \to$
$0.75s + 9 - 9 = 30 - 9 \to$
$0.75s = 21 \to \dfrac{0.75s}{0.75} = \dfrac{21}{0.75} \to s = 28$
$w = 60 - s = 60 - 28 = 32$

38. $x \le 2$ $\quad 7x - 6 - 2x \le 2x + 4 - 2x \to$
$5x - 6 \le 4 \to 5x - 6 + 6 \le 4 + 6 \to$
$5x \le 10 \to \dfrac{5x}{5} \le \dfrac{10}{5} \to x \le 2$

39. B The "less than" part of the inequality indicates shading to the left; the "or equal to" part indicates that the endpoint is a solid dot.

40. A $\quad 0.35m + 0.65 \ge 4.50 \to$
$0.35m + 0.65 - 0.65 \ge 4.50 - 0.65 \to$
$0.35m \ge 3.85 \to$
$\dfrac{0.35m}{0.35} \ge \dfrac{3.85}{0.35} \to m \ge 11$

41. B Replacing x with 11 in each of the inequalities and evaluating produces the following results:

A. $28 < -18$ B. $74 \ge -24$
C. $45 \le 36$ D. $12 > 27$

42. $y = \dfrac{c - ax}{b}$ $\quad ax + by = c \to$
$ax + by - ax = c - ax \to$
$by = c - ax \to$
$\dfrac{by}{b} = \dfrac{c - ax}{b} \to$
$y = \dfrac{c - ax}{b}$

43. C $\quad 5p + 135 \le 400 \to$
$5p + 135 - 135 \le 400 - 135 \to$
$5p \le 265 \to$
$\dfrac{5p}{5} \le \dfrac{265}{5} \to p \le 53$

44. D $\quad x + 19 < 15 \to$
$x + 19 - 19 < 15 - 19 \to$
$x < -4$

45. $x \ge 4$ $\quad 2x - 4(x + 3) \ge 4 + 3(4 - 3x) \to$
$2x - 4x - 12 \ge 4 + 12 - 9x \to$
$-2x - 12 \ge 16 - 9x \to$
$-2x - 12 + 9x \ge 16 - 9x + 9x \to$
$7x - 12 \ge 16 \to$
$7x - 12 + 12 \ge 16 + 12 \to$
$7x \ge 28 \to$
$\dfrac{7x}{7} \ge \dfrac{28}{7} \to$
$x \ge 4$

46. C Buying g gallons of gas at $3.15 per gallon incurs a cost of 3.15g$. This is added to $1.65 to get the total, $40.71.

47. 86 $\quad 5f + 150 = 580 \to$
$5f + 150 - 150 = 580 - 150 \to$
$\dfrac{5f}{5} = \dfrac{430}{5} \to$
$f = 86$

48. $x < 4$

$5(x - 6) < 2(x - 9) \rightarrow$
$5x - 30 < 2x - 18 \rightarrow$
$5x - 30 - 2x < 2x - 18 - 2x \rightarrow$
$3x - 30 < -18 \rightarrow$
$3x - 30 + 30 < -18 + 30 \rightarrow$
$3x < 12 \rightarrow \dfrac{3x}{3} < \dfrac{12}{3} \rightarrow x < 4$

49. $x = 2$ or
$x = -\dfrac{3}{2}$

$2x^2 - 7x + 6 = 0 \rightarrow$
$(2x + 3)(x - 2) = 0 \rightarrow$
$2x + 3 = 0$ or $x - 2 = 0 \rightarrow$
$2x = -3$ or $x = 2 \rightarrow$
$x = -\dfrac{3}{2}$ or $x = 2$

50. **8 seconds**
When the rock reaches the bottom of the cliff, $D = 1024$:

$1024 = 16t^2 \rightarrow \dfrac{1024}{16} = \dfrac{16t^2}{16} \rightarrow$

$64 = t^2 \rightarrow \pm\sqrt{64} = \sqrt{t^2} \rightarrow$
$\pm 8 = t$.

Disregarding the negative time value, $t = 8$.

Chapter 11 Graphing Equations

1.

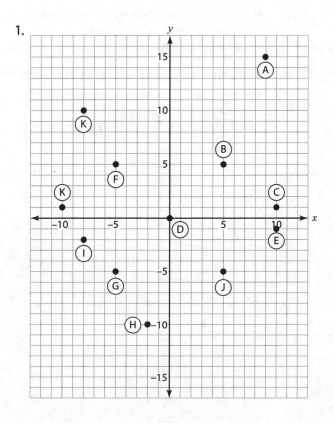

2. You can calculate the slopes, or you can solve this by remembering that positive sloped lines go up to the right, and lines steeper than 45 degrees have slopes whose absolute value is greater than 1.

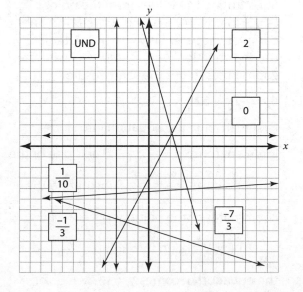

3. **D**   Only line D has a slope that is the negative reciprocal of the given line. It is perpendicular to the given line. It is the only one that we can be *sure* is part of a right triangle.

4. $\frac{2}{3}$ Using the point (3, 2), we find that $b = 18$. Substituting 4 for x, we get 16 and see that the y value must be $\frac{2}{3}$ to satisfy the equation.

5. **B**   The curve is a simple cubic function.

6. **D**   This line has the required slope.

7. **B**   Only these coordinates satisfy the equation.

8. **A**   Plotting the other curve on these axes yields the answer.

9. **A**   The plot for investment A has a steeper slope and will outpace the other investment.

10. **No**   The slopes between any two points are not equal as they should be on a line.

11. $y = -x + 2$

    The slope between the points is –1. Substituting the values from the point $(-3, 5)$ into $y = -x + b$ leads us to $b = 2$. The complete equation is $y = -x + 2$. Alternately, use the equation $y - y_1 = -m(x - x_1)$ with the coordinates to get the same result.

12. $6y = -7x + 62$

    First rearrange the equation into slope-intercept form: $y = \frac{6}{7}x - \frac{8}{7}$. The slope of the perpendicular line is $-\frac{7}{6}$. Substituting the coordinates of the point, $y = -\frac{7}{6}x + b = 1 = -\frac{7}{6}(8) + b$. Working through $b = \frac{31}{3}$, the equation becomes $y = -\frac{7}{6}x + \frac{31}{3}$ or $6y = -7x + 62$.

13. $f(x) = \frac{x^3}{x - 2}$

    The equation in the table is linear, while the given function is approximately a square function. The given function will increase faster.

14. $5x - 4y = 25$

    A line parallel to the given one must have the same slope. We do not want to change the left side of the equation. To be on a line, a point's coordinates must make the equation true. Substituting (9, 5) into $5x - 4y = b$ yields $b = 25$, and the completed equation is $5x - 4y = 25$.

15. $-\frac{1}{4}$ The slope of a perpendicular line must be the negative reciprocal.

16. **D**   These are arranged in order of increasing slope.

17. **B**   The speed decreases with distance, meaning the body is slowing.

18. **B**   It is moving faster than the body in the graph. Note that the axes have traded their usual positions.

19. **B**   Starting with $y = mx + b$, replace m with the slope and x and y with the point's coordinates. Solving gives $b = 4$. Rearranging the equation gives the answer.

20.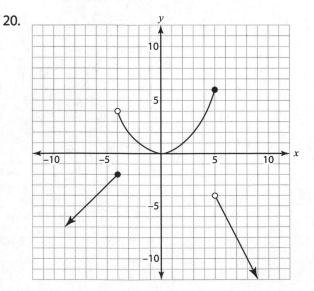

21. **10**

22. $f(x) = 3x^2 - 6x + 8$

    The equation of a second order curve, given the vertex and one point, can be found using $f(x) = a(x - h)^2 + k$, where h and k are the coordinates of the vertex. Substituting $(1, 5)$ gives $f(x) = a(x - 1)^2 + 5$. Next, substitute the coordinates $(0, 8)$ for x and $f(x)$. Solve for a. With $a = 3$, expand the equation and collect like terms to get the answer.

23. $y = 2x$

    The relationship is approximate but very close to a best fit in the data. The minor differences are "noise" one expects in real-world measurements.

24. The line between $(-1, -4)$ and $(1, 7)$ is steeper. Its slope is $5\frac{1}{2}$, while the slope for the equation is 5.

25. **A** The equation has the same behavior as a quadratic.

26. **B** Slope is also defined as rise divided by run, where rise is vertical and run horizontal. This division gives the correct answer.

27.

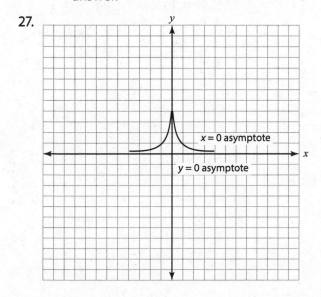

28. **max $y \approx 60$**

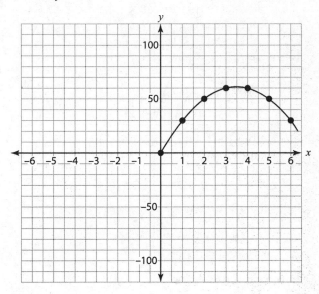

29. $y = 11x - 26$

    The slope of the line is 11. We start with $y = 11x + b$. Substituting the coordinates of either point, we get $b = -26$. We use the other point's coordinates to check our work.

30. $3b + 4n = 24$

    The price of one type of book times the number of that type of book is the subtotal for that type of book. Add the two subtotals to get the total cost.

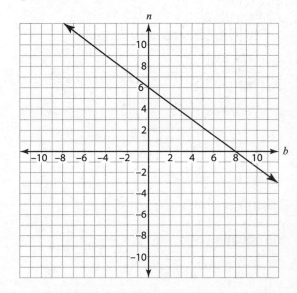

31.

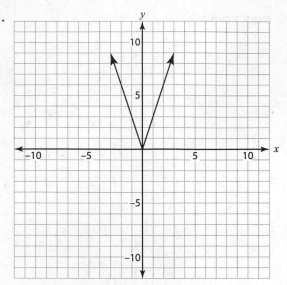

33.

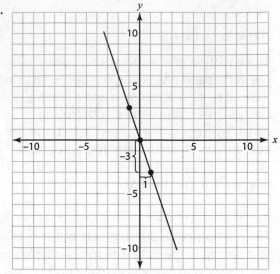

32. max *p* ≈ 44

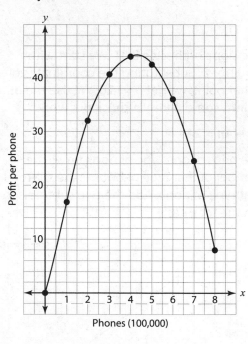

Phones (100,000)

34.

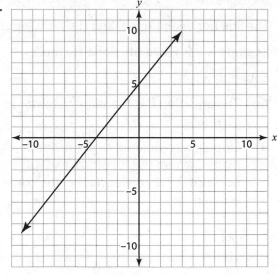

35.

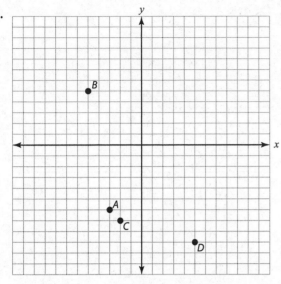

36. The rocket with trajectory given by the equation goes higher.

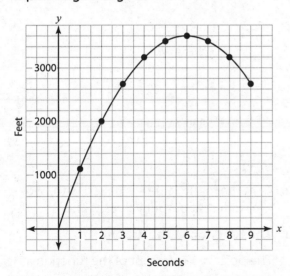

37. **A** This is a positive quadratic and has these end behaviors.

38. **(0, −4); (0, −2); (0, 8)**

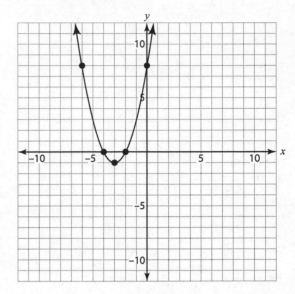

39. **D** Only the circle will look the same if we put a mirror on the *x* −axis.

40. **(−3, +9)**

Points symmetric to the origin have the opposite coordinates.

41. **C** The end behavior is determined by the highest order factor, which here is a cubic.

42. **A** and **C**

43. $\dfrac{3}{5}$ Here, count the change in *y* and divide by the change in *x* between the same two points.

44. **Yes** Using the slope formula shows that the slope of the line through the two points is the same as the given slope.

45. **A** and **D**

They have the same slopes.

46. **In order from left to right: D, C, B.**

47.

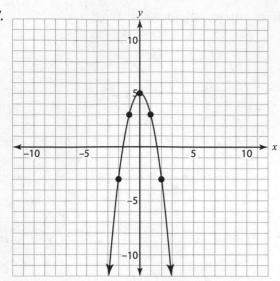

48. $y = -\dfrac{2}{3}x + \dfrac{27}{3}$ or $3y + 2x = 27$

Starting with the slope of $m = -\dfrac{2}{3}$ and using either $y = mx + b$ or $(y - y_1) = -m(x - x_1)$ with the coordinates of the point gives the answer.

49. **(2, 4)**

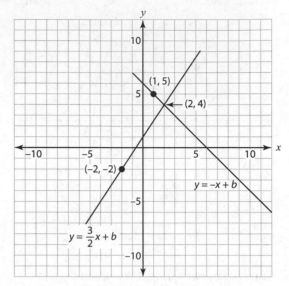

50. **D**   This is an inverted quadratic.

Chapter 12 Functions

1. The graph of a proportional relationship is a line passing through the origin. The unit rate is the slope of the line.

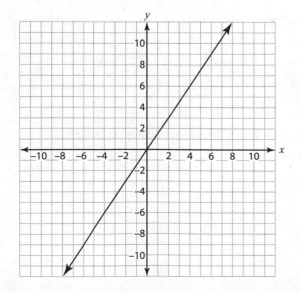

2. **C**   The input value 4 is paired with two different output values, 3 and 7.

3. **The function in the graph.**

   The positive x-intercept of the function in the graph is slightly larger than 6. The other function has an x-intercept found by setting $y = 0$ and solving for x: $0 = 7x + 24 \rightarrow$ $x = \dfrac{24}{7} = 3\dfrac{3}{7}$.

4. **B** $3x - 5y = 9$ may be put in the form $y = mx + b$ by solving for y. Solving any of the other equations for y would not result in an equation in that form.

5. **A**   The function is increasing over the parts of the x-axis where y-values go up as x moves from left to right.

6. **C**   If $f(x) = \frac{1}{2}x + 1$, then $f(12) = \frac{1}{2} \cdot 12 + 1 =$ $6 + 1 = 7$. Substituting 12 for x into any other of the functions produces a value other than 7.

7. **–2** $f(-7) = \frac{2}{5} \cdot (-7) + \frac{4}{5} = \frac{-14}{5} + \frac{4}{5} =$ $\frac{-10}{5} = -2$

8. **D**   Only the numbers 0, 1, 2, 3, … can be used to count people in this situation. These are the non-negative integers.

9. **$f(x) = -2x + 10$**

     The initial value in the graph is 7. The initial value of $f(x) = -2x + 10$ is 10.

10. **B**   If folded along the y-axis, the halves of the graph would coincide. This is characteristic of symmetry about the y-axis.

11. **A**   Algebraic expressions with variables raised to powers typically do not represent linear functions.

12. **D**   Any such number may be used to denote elapsed time.

13. **taxi**   The rate for the train is the difference between any two d-values spaced 1 hour apart, at 30 miles per hour. The rate for the taxi is the multiplier in the expression $40t + 5$, 40 miles per hour.

14. **(4, 2), (4, –2)**

     Any two ordered pairs where the y-values are opposites and x is the square of y will suffice, for instance (100, 10), (100, –10), or $\left(\frac{9}{4}, \frac{3}{2}\right), \left(\frac{9}{4}, -\frac{3}{2}\right)$, or (6.25, 2.5), (6.25, –2.5).

15. The graph is a line. Find any two points on the line by substituting values for x. For instance, if $x = 0$, $f(x) = -\frac{3}{2} \cdot 0 + 8 = 8$, so (0, 8) is a point; if $x = 4$, $f(x) = -\frac{3}{2} \cdot 4 + 8 = 2$, so (4, 2) is another.

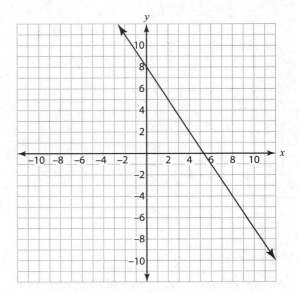

16. **12** $f(-3) = -2(-3)^2 - 7(-3) + 9 =$ $-2 \cdot 9 + 21 + 9 = -18 + 30 = 12$

17. **$f(x)$**   For $g(x)$, $m = -3$. The slope of $f(x)$ can be found by using the slope formula on any two points from the table. Using the rightmost two columns, $m = \frac{15 - 7}{9 - 5} = \frac{8}{4} = 2$. $2 > -3$, so $f(x)$ has the larger slope.

18. **$g(x)$**   The minimum in the graph of $g(x)$ is the y-value of the vertex, –6. The minimum for $f(x)$ is $f\left(-\frac{b}{2a}\right)$, where $a = 1$ and $b = -8$. $-\frac{b}{2a} = -\frac{-8}{2 \cdot 1} = 4$, and $f(4) =$ $4^2 - 8 \cdot 4 + 8 = 16 - 32 + 8 = -8$. $-6 > -8$, so $g(x)$ has the larger minimum.

19. **D**   If the graph is folded on the diagonal, the parts of the graph on either side of the fold would not coincide.

20. Due to the symmetry of the graph of a quadratic function, the points (–1, 2) and (9, –3) are also on the graph and may be used for the sketch.

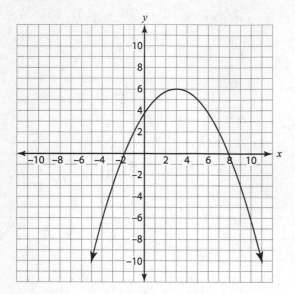

21. **$x \geq -5$**

    The x-values of the points of the graph make up the domain. Points on this graph have x-values larger than or equal to –5.

22. **8**   The y-value must be the same for all occurrences of $x = -3$.

23. **4%** $R(400) = \dfrac{2000}{400 + 100} = \dfrac{2000}{500} = 4$

24. **Jimmy**

    Jimmy's rate is 3.95 feet per second. Kenny's rate can be found by using the slope formula with any two pairs from the table: $m = \dfrac{78 - 39}{20 - 10} =$ $\dfrac{39}{10} = 3.9$ feet per second, slower than Jimmy.

25. **A**   If $g(x)$ has only one x-intercept, it must be the vertex, $x = -\dfrac{b}{2a}$, with $a = 1$ and $b = -2$: $x = -\dfrac{-2}{2 \cdot 1} = 1$. This is between the x-intercepts of $f(x)$, 3 and –3.

26. **17** $f(-6) = \dfrac{5}{9}(-6)^2 - \dfrac{2}{3} \cdot (-6) - 7 =$

    $\dfrac{5}{9} \cdot 36 + 4 - 7 = 20 - 3 = 17$

27. **the chute**

    The chute is emptying the hopper at the rate of 5 kilograms per second, the rate in the linear function. The truck dumps at the rate of of $\dfrac{125}{30} = 4\dfrac{1}{6}$ kilograms per second.

28. **A**   The steeper line indicates a faster rate of part stamping.

29. Note: There is no reason to connect the dots. Doing so would imply there are more domain values than are displayed in the table. For instance, joining the points (2, 6) and (5, 2) with a segment would mean that there are points whose x-values are 3 and 4, but there are no such points.

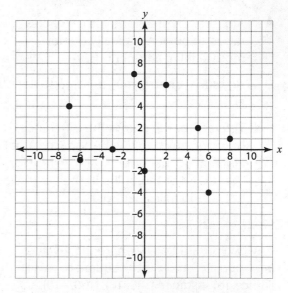

30. **2nd line**

    The y-intercept of the first line is 17; its slope is –3. The equation is $y = -3x + 17$. The x-intercept occurs where $y = 0$: $0 = -3x + 17 \rightarrow 3x = 17 \rightarrow x = \dfrac{17}{3}$. Likewise for the second line: $5x - 3 \cdot 0 = 30 \rightarrow 5x = 30 \rightarrow x = 6$. The second line has the larger x-intercept.

31. **C** The function is in the form $f(x) = mx + b$, the form of a linear function.

32. **243** An element from D may be assigned to any of the 3 elements of R. The elements in the range may be reused, so there are 3 options for assigning the next element from D, and 3 for the next, and the next, and the last. The total number of assignments, or functions, is $3 \cdot 3 \cdot 3 \cdot 3 \cdot 3 = 243$.

33. **{–7, –6, –3, –1, 0, 2, 5, 6, 8}**

    The domain is the set of input, or x-values.

34. **C** The function doesn't tell what an individual person should request or seek for a salary, and it doesn't address how much *more* is earned under any circumstance.

35. **–2 < x < 5**

    A function is constant where its graph is horizontal.

36. **f(x)** The slope of $f(x)$ is –3. The slope of $g(x)$ is found with the slope formula:

    $m = \dfrac{-5 - 0}{0 - 7} = \dfrac{-5}{-7} = \dfrac{5}{7}$. Even though the

    slope of $g(x)$ is greater that the slope of $f(x)$, $f(x)$ is steeper because the absolute value is greater.

37. **later**

    The table shows a height of 0 when $t = 15$. To find the time according to the function, set $h(t) = 0$ and solve for t: $0 = -16t^2 + 320t \rightarrow$ $0 = -16t(t - 20) \rightarrow -16t = 0$ or $t - 20 = 0 \rightarrow$ $t = 0$ or $t = 20$. The value $t = 0$ corresponds to a height of 0 when the object is launched. According to the function, the object falls to the ground at $t = 20$, later than indicated by the telemetry.

38. **(a, b)**

    Plotting the ordered pairs (a, b) for which $f(a) = b$ is how the graph of the function $f(x)$ is produced.

39. $x < \dfrac{5}{2}$

    The function is negative when $f(x) < 0$:
    $\dfrac{5}{8}x - \dfrac{25}{16} < 0 \rightarrow \dfrac{5}{8}x < \dfrac{25}{16} \rightarrow$
    $\dfrac{8}{5} \cdot \dfrac{5}{8}x < \dfrac{8}{5} \cdot \dfrac{25}{16} \rightarrow x < \dfrac{5}{2}$

40. **–3 < x < 5**

    The function is positive when the graph is above the x-axis.

41. **the graph**

    The line in the graph has slope
    $m = \dfrac{200 - 0}{10 - 0} = 20$.
    The values in the table have a rate of change
    $m = \dfrac{90 - 54}{5 - 3} = \dfrac{36}{2} = 18$.

42. **not a function**

    The graph fails the vertical line test, showing that there are input values associated with more than a single output value. For instance, there are three y-values associated with $x = 0$: –5, 0, and 5.

43. **21** $f\left(-\dfrac{3}{2}\right) = 4\left(-\dfrac{3}{2}\right)^2 - 6\left(-\dfrac{3}{2}\right) + 3 =$

    $4 \cdot \dfrac{9}{4} + 3 \cdot 3 + 3 = 9 + 9 + 3 = 21$

44. **–9 ≤ x < 0, 2 < x ≤ 8**

    The x-values of the points of the graph make up the domain. Points on this graph have x-values between –9 and 0, including –9 but not 0, and between 2 and 8, including 8 but not 2.

45. **g(x)** $f(x)$ is negative over the interval $-4 < x < 7$, a segment of length $7 - (-4) = 11$. $g(x)$ is negative over the interval $-8 < x < 4$, a segment of length $4 - (-8) = 12$.

46. **yes** The graph passes the vertical test: every vertical line crosses the graph no more than once.

47. the y-intercept

The y-intercept is $f(0)$: $f(0) = -\dfrac{9}{10} \cdot 0 + 9 = 9$.

The x-intercept is where $f(x) = 0$:

$0 = -\dfrac{9}{10}x + 9 \rightarrow \dfrac{9}{10}x = 9 \rightarrow$

$\dfrac{10}{9} \cdot \dfrac{9}{10}x = \dfrac{10}{9} \cdot 9 \rightarrow x = 10$.

48. Make a table of x-y pairs, substituting x-values in the function and computing y-values. Here is a partial table:

x	–2	0	2	3	5
f(x)	0	–5	–9	–8	–0

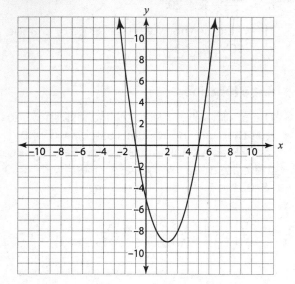

49. 260 feet

$h(t) = -16 \cdot 4^2 + 128 \cdot 4 + 4 =$

$-16 \cdot 16 + 512 + 4 =$

$-256 + 516 = 260$

50. $0 \le t \le 4 + \dfrac{1}{2}\sqrt{65}$

The ball is not hit until $t = 0$, so values of t less than 0 aren't in the domain. Also values of t corresponding to the time after the ball comes back down are not in the domain. To find these values, set $h(t) = 0$ and solve for t: $-16t^2 + 128t + 4 = 0 \rightarrow -4(4t^2 - 32t - 1) = 0 \rightarrow 4t^2 - 32t - 1 = 0$. This last equation can't be factored, so use the quadratic formula with $a = 4$, $b = -32$, and $c = -1$:

$t = \dfrac{-(-32) \pm \sqrt{(-32)^2 - 4 \cdot 4 \cdot (-1)}}{2 \cdot 4} =$

$\dfrac{32 \pm \sqrt{1024 + 16}}{8} = \dfrac{32 \pm \sqrt{1024 + 16}}{8} =$

$\dfrac{32 \pm \sqrt{1040}}{8} = \dfrac{32 \pm \sqrt{16 \cdot 65}}{8} = \dfrac{32 \pm 4\sqrt{65}}{8} =$

$\dfrac{32}{8} \pm \dfrac{4\sqrt{65}}{8} = 4 \pm \dfrac{1}{2}\sqrt{65}$.

Using the minus sign gives a negative value for t, so $t = 4 + \dfrac{1}{2}\sqrt{65} \approx 8.03$, which is the upper value of the domain.

Mathematical Reasoning

50 questions | **90 minutes**

This posttest is intended to give you an idea of how ready you are to take the real GED® Mathematical Reasoning test. Try to work every problem, in a quiet area and with enough time so that you are free from distractions. The usual time allotted for the test is 90 minutes, but it is more important to be sure you get a chance to think about every problem than it is to finish ahead of time.

Answers and solutions for every problem can be found at the end of the posttest.

1. If the table represents a function, fill in the two missing numbers. *Write your answers in the shaded boxes.*

x	−2	−1	0	1	2	1	5	−2
f(x)		3	0	2	6		7	5

2. Circle any pair of points on the graph that show why it is not the graph of a function.

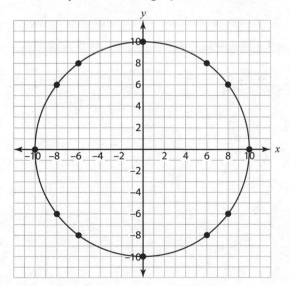

3. If $f(x) = 2x^2 + 7x + 3$, what is $f(5)$?

   A. 88
   B. 63
   C. 138
   D. 85

4. Circle two points on the number line that are separated by a distance of 23 units.

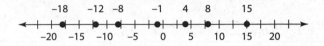

5. Multiply $\left(x^{-\frac{1}{3}} \right)\left(x^{\frac{1}{3}} \right)$.

   A. 1
   B. $x^{-\frac{1}{9}}$
   C. $x^{\frac{2}{3}}$
   D. $x^{-\frac{2}{3}}$

6. Factor $8x^2 + 24x + 18$.

   A. $(4x + 3)^2$
   B. $2(2x + 3)^2$
   C. $(4x + 3)(2x + 6)$
   D. $(2x + 3)^2$

7. Divide $\dfrac{x^2 - 9x + 20}{x - 5}$.

   A. $\dfrac{x - 4}{x - 5}$
   B. 1
   C. $\dfrac{x - 5}{x - 4}$
   D. $x - 4$

8. Solve for x: $3x - 11 < 5x - 7$.

   A. $x > -2$
   B. $x < -2$
   C. $x > 2$
   D. $x < 2$

9. Divide $\dfrac{x^{-2}y^5}{x^{-3}y^2}$.

   A. $\dfrac{y^3}{x^5}$

   B. xy^3

   C. $\dfrac{x^5}{y^3}$

   D. $x^{-5}y^7$

10. Solve for x: $4x^2 - 7x = 15$.

    A. $\left\{ -\dfrac{5}{4}, 3 \right\}$

    B. $\left\{ \dfrac{5}{4}, -3 \right\}$

    C. $\left\{ -\dfrac{5}{4}, -3 \right\}$

    D. $\left\{ \dfrac{5}{4}, 3 \right\}$

11. Divide $\dfrac{x^2y^4z^{-3}}{xyz^3}$.

    A. $\dfrac{x^2y^4}{xyz^6}$

    B. $\dfrac{x}{y^3z^6}$

    C. $\dfrac{xy^3}{z^6}$

    D. $\dfrac{xy^3}{z^9}$

12. Circle all values that are solutions to
    $4x^2 - 36 = 0$.

    -36 -9 -3 3 9 36

13. Solve for x: $5x - 1 > 8x - 7$.

    A. $x > -2$
    B. $x < -2$
    C. $x > 2$
    D. $x < 2$

14. Circle the correct mathematical symbol, $<$, $>$,
    or $=$.

$>$	$>$	$>$	$>$
$3 < 5$	$-8 < -9$	$-9 < 5$	$12 < 12$
$=$	$=$	$=$	$=$

15. Write $\dfrac{136}{32}$ as a mixed number in lowest terms.

    A. $\dfrac{17}{4}$

    B. $4\dfrac{1}{4}$

    C. $4\dfrac{8}{32}$

    D. $4\dfrac{4}{16}$

16. Solve for x: $4x^2 - 9 = 0$.

    A. $\pm\sqrt{\dfrac{9}{4}}$

    B. $\pm\dfrac{3}{2}$

    C. $\pm\dfrac{2}{3}$

    D. $\pm\sqrt{\dfrac{3}{2}}$

17. Add $7\dfrac{3}{8} + 4\dfrac{2}{5}$.

    Write your answer in the space below.

18. Subtract $\dfrac{2x-7}{4x} - \dfrac{7y+3}{6y}$.

   A. $\dfrac{9xy-4}{24xy}$

   B. $-\dfrac{6x+8xy+21y}{12xy}$

   C. $\dfrac{-8xy-21y+6x}{12xy}$

   D. $\dfrac{2x-7y-10xy}{24xy}$

19. Fill in the blank: $7:4::49:\underline{\hspace{1cm}}$.

20. The ratio of the sides of two squares is 1:2. What is the ratio of their areas?

   A. 1:1
   B. 1:2
   C. 1:4
   D. 2:1

21. Add $13.50 + 17.995 + 6.008$. *Write your answer in the box.*

   [ ]

22. Circle the number of the straight line that has slope 4 and that passes through the point (5, 3).

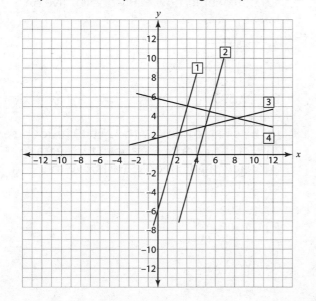

23. What does $f(x)$ approach as x becomes larger and larger but negative, if

   $f(x) = x^3 - 2x^2 + 12x + 5$? *Circle the correct answer.*

   $+\infty$

   0

   $-\infty$

24. What fraction equals 0.875?

   A. $\dfrac{87.5}{100}$

   B. $\dfrac{151}{200}$

   C. $\dfrac{7}{8}$

   D. $\dfrac{7}{80}$

25. Write 0.0095 as a reduced fraction. *Write your answer in the box.*

   [ ]

26. What fraction equals 17.5%? *Write your answer in the box.*

   [ ]

27. Arrange in order from greatest to smallest: 0.0012, 0.00067, 0.0023, 0.01, 0.009

   $\underline{\hspace{1.5cm}} > \underline{\hspace{1.5cm}} > \underline{\hspace{1.5cm}} > \underline{\hspace{1.5cm}} >$

   $\underline{\hspace{1.5cm}}$

28. What is the perimeter of a hexagon that is 17 inches on a side?

   A. 51 inches
   B. 102 inches
   C. 112 inches
   D. 119 inches

29. What is the area of this triangle?

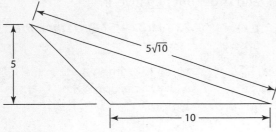

A. 50
B. 25
C. 10
D. 5

30. What is the length of a side of a right triangle if the other side measures 12 centimeters and the hypotenuse measures 20 centimeters?

A. 8 centimeters
B. 16 centimeters
C. 23.32 centimeters
D. 256 centimeters

31. Which of the following has a larger area?

_____ a circle with a diameter of 30 centimeters

_____ a square that measures 30 centimeters on a side

32. Gerald uses 4 cups of flour and 1 cup of sugar in his famous cookie recipe. If he needs to make five batches, how much flour and sugar must he have on hand?

A. 4 cups flour, 1 cup sugar

B. 10 cups flour, $2\frac{1}{2}$ cups sugar

C. 5 cups flour, 20 cups sugar
D. 20 cups flour, 5 cups sugar

33. Fill in the blank: 9 : 5 :: _____ : 75.

34. Evaluate $4^{\frac{5}{2}}$.

A. 32
B. 1.74
C. 512
D. 1,048,567

35. Divide $\dfrac{\frac{3}{5}}{\frac{5}{3}}$.

A. 1

B. $\dfrac{6}{10}$

C. $\dfrac{5}{15}$

D. $\dfrac{9}{25}$

36. When tossing a fair coin, what is the probability of tossing two heads in two throws?

A. 1

B. $\dfrac{1}{2}$

C. $\dfrac{1}{4}$

D. 0

37. Only 9% of the residents in a county live on farms. If the population of the county is 127,000 people, how many do NOT live on farms?

A. 11,430
B. 14,111
C. 114,300
D. 115,570

38. In the same county, with 127,000 residents, 17% of the people are above the average age. How many people are above the average age?

A. 21,590
B. 74,700
C. 90,170
D. 105,050

39. A bowl is filled with 5 red, 6 yellow, and 4 white balls. What is the probability of drawing a red ball and then a white ball at random?

    A. $\dfrac{9}{21}$

    B. $\dfrac{9}{29}$

    C. $\dfrac{2}{21}$

    D. $\dfrac{1}{3}$

40. Expand $(2x + 5)^2$.

    A. $4x^2 + 25$
    B. $2x^2 + 10x + 5$
    C. $4x + 10$
    D. $4x^2 + 20x + 25$

41. What is the smallest integer value that makes $x \geq -10$ true? *Write your answer in the box.*

42. Arrange in order from smallest to greatest:

    0.47, 21%, 0.06, $\dfrac{4}{5}$, $\dfrac{3}{8}$, $33\dfrac{1}{3}\%$

    _____ < _____ < _____ < _____ <

    _____ < _____

43. A line has the equation $3x - 5y = 15$. What is its slope?

    A. $-\dfrac{5}{3}$

    B. $-\dfrac{3}{5}$

    C. $\dfrac{3}{5}$

    D. $\dfrac{5}{3}$

44. What is the sum of $2x + 13$ and $6x + 3$? *Write your answer in the box.*

45. Given a group of 12 women and 6 men, what is the probability of picking 4 men and no women at random?

    A. $\dfrac{1}{3}$

    B. $\dfrac{1}{16}$

    C. $\dfrac{1}{81}$

    D. $\dfrac{1}{204}$

46. Graph $y = -x^2 + 2x + 8$.

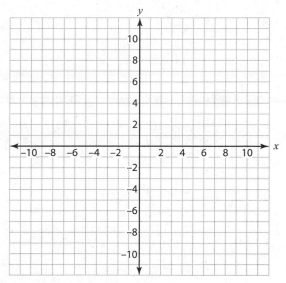

47. What is the probability of throwing a 3 with a fair six-sided die?

    A. $\dfrac{1}{3}$

    B. $\dfrac{1}{4}$

    C. $\dfrac{1}{6}$

    D. $\dfrac{1}{12}$

48. If the enrollment at a school was 1250 last year and is 1500 this year, what is the percent increase from last year to this year?

    A. 20%
    B. 17%
    C. 9%
    D. −20%

49. Build the equation of the line passing between the points $(2, 7)$ and $(4, -7)$ by filling in the blanks with the correct numbers. Choose from −21, −14, −7, 7, 14, 21. (*Note*: On the real GED test, you will click on the numbers you choose and "drag" them into position.)

    $y = $ _____ $x + $ _____

50. Where does the graph of $y = 6x^2 + 5x - 6$ intersect the *y*-axis?

    A. 1
    B. 6
    C. −6
    D. −1

THIS IS THE END OF THE MATHEMATICAL REASONING POSTTEST.

ANSWERS AND SOLUTIONS BEGIN ON THE NEXT PAGE.

Answers and Solutions

1. **5 and 2**   A function has only one $f(x)$ value for each x. The missing numbers must match those already in the chart.

x	−2	−1	0	1	2	1	5	−2
f(x)	5	3	0	2	6	2	7	5

2. **(6, 8)** and **(6, −8)**   Any point on the top half of the circle and the point directly below it on the lower half of the circle will suffice; for instance (−8, 6) and (−8, −6), or (0, 10) and (0, −10) also work.

3. **A** $f(5) = 2(5)^2 + 7(5) + 3 =$
$2 \cdot 25 + 35 + 3 = 50 + 38 = 88$

4. **−8 and 15** $|15 - (-8)| = |15 + 8| = |23| = 23$

5. **A** $\left(x^{-\frac{1}{3}}\right)\left(x^{\frac{1}{3}}\right) = x^{-\frac{1}{3}+\frac{1}{3}} = x^0 = 1$

6. **B** $8x^2 + 24x + 18 =$
$2(4x^2 + 12x + 9) =$
$2(2x + 3)(2x + 3) =$
$2(2x + 3)^2$

7. **D**   Factor and cancel:
$$\frac{x^2 - 9x + 20}{x - 5} =$$
$$\frac{(x - 4)(x - 5)}{x - 5} =$$
$$x - 4$$

8. **A** $3x - 11 < 5x - 7 \rightarrow$
$3x - 11 - 5x < 5x - 7 - 5x \rightarrow$
$-2x - 11 < -7 \rightarrow$
$-2x - 11 + 11 < -7 + 11 \rightarrow$
$-2x < 4 \rightarrow$
$\frac{-2x}{-2} > \frac{4}{-2} \rightarrow x > -2$

9. **B**   Rearranging before dividing:
$$\frac{x^{-2}y^5}{x^{-3}y^2} = \frac{x^3 y^5}{x^2 y^2} = xy^3$$

10. **A** $4x^2 - 7x - 15 = 15 - 15 \rightarrow$
$4x^2 - 7x - 15 = 0 \rightarrow$
$(4x + 5)(x - 3) = 0 \rightarrow$
$4x + 5 = 0$ or $x - 3 = 0 \rightarrow$
$4x + 5 - 5 = 0 - 5$
or $x - 3 + 3 = 0 + 3 \rightarrow$
$4x = -5$ or $x = 3 \rightarrow$
$\frac{4x}{4} = \frac{-5}{4}$ or $x = 3 \rightarrow$
$x = -\frac{5}{4}$ or $x = 3$

11. **C**   Rearranging first, $\frac{x^2 y^4}{xyz^3 z^3} = \frac{xy^3}{z^6}$.

12. **−3 and 3**   Since the term with x^1 is missing, solve for x^2:
$4x^2 - 36 + 36 = 0 + 36 \rightarrow$
$4x^2 = 36 \rightarrow$
$\frac{4x^2}{4} = \frac{36}{4} \rightarrow$
$x^2 = 9$

Now use the square root property:
$\sqrt{x^2} = \pm\sqrt{9} \rightarrow x = \pm 3$

13. **D** $5x - 1 > 8x - 7 \rightarrow$
$5x - 1 - 8x > 8x - 7 - 8x \rightarrow$
$-3x - 1 > -7 \rightarrow$
$-3x - 1 + 1 > -7 + 1 \rightarrow$
$-3x > -6 \rightarrow$
$\frac{-3x}{-3} < \frac{-6}{-3} \rightarrow x < 2$

14. In order left to right the following should be circled: **<, >, <, =**

15. **B** $\frac{136}{32} = 4\frac{8}{32} = 4\frac{1}{4}$

16. **B** $4x^2 - 9 = 0 \rightarrow 4x^2 = 9 \rightarrow$

$\dfrac{4x^2}{4} = \dfrac{9}{4} \rightarrow x^2 = \dfrac{9}{4} \rightarrow$

$\sqrt{x^2} = \pm\sqrt{\dfrac{9}{4}} \rightarrow$

$x = \pm\dfrac{3}{2}$

17. $11\dfrac{31}{40}$ $7 + 4 = 11$ and $\dfrac{3}{8} + \dfrac{2}{5} =$

$\dfrac{5}{5} \cdot \dfrac{3}{8} + \dfrac{8}{8} \cdot \dfrac{2}{5} = \dfrac{15}{40} + \dfrac{16}{40} = \dfrac{31}{40}$

18. **B** The least common denominator is $12xy$.

$\dfrac{2x-7}{4x} - \dfrac{7y+3}{6y} =$

$\dfrac{3y}{3y} \cdot \dfrac{2x-7}{4x} - \dfrac{2x}{2x} \cdot \dfrac{7y+3}{6y} =$

$\dfrac{6xy - 21y}{12xy} - \dfrac{14xy + 6x}{12xy} =$

$\dfrac{6xy - 21y - 14xy - 6x}{12xy} =$

$\dfrac{-8xy - 21y - 6x}{12xy} = -\dfrac{6x + 8xy + 21y}{12xy}$

19. **28** $\dfrac{7}{4} = \dfrac{49}{n} \rightarrow 4n \cdot \dfrac{7}{4} = 4n \cdot \dfrac{49}{n} \rightarrow$

$7n = 4 \cdot 49 \rightarrow \dfrac{7n}{7} = \dfrac{4 \cdot 49}{7} \rightarrow$

$n = 4 \cdot 7 \rightarrow n = 28$

20. **C** Although the ratio of sides is 1:2, we square sides to find area, so the ratio of areas is 1:4.

21. **37.503**

22. **line 2**

23. **−∞** The highest-degree term rules the end behavior.

24. **C** $0.875 = \dfrac{875}{1000} = \dfrac{7}{8}$

25. $\dfrac{19}{2000}$ $\dfrac{95}{10,000} = \dfrac{19}{2000}$

26. $\dfrac{7}{40}$ $17.5\% = 0.175 = \dfrac{175}{1000} = \dfrac{7}{40}$

27. **0.01 > 0.009 > 0.0023 > 0.0012 > 0.00067**

28. **B** Hexagons have six sides, so $p = 6 \times 17 = 102$.

29. **B** The area of a triangle is given by $A = \dfrac{1}{2}bh = \dfrac{1}{2} \cdot 10 \cdot 5 = 5 \cdot 5 = 25$.

30. **B** Use the Pythagorean theorem.

$a^2 + 12^2 = 20^2 \rightarrow$

$a^2 + 144 = 400 \rightarrow$

$a^2 + 144 - 144 = 400 - 144 \rightarrow$

$a^2 = 256 \rightarrow \sqrt{a^2} = \sqrt{256} \rightarrow$

$a = 16$

31. **the square**

Since the diameter of the circle is equal to the length of a side of the square, the circle fits within the square, so it is smaller. Or you can calculate the areas, using a circle radius of 15.

32. **D** The flour/sugar ratio of 4:1 is for one batch, and 4:1::20:5.

33. **135** $\dfrac{9}{5} = \dfrac{n}{75} \rightarrow 75 \cdot \dfrac{9}{5} = 75 \cdot \dfrac{n}{75} \rightarrow$

$15 \cdot 9 = n \rightarrow 135 = n$

34. **A** By the properties of exponents,

$4^{\frac{5}{2}} = \left(\sqrt{4}\right)^5 = 2^5 = 32$.

35. **D** Invert the denominator and multiply:

$\dfrac{3}{5} \times \dfrac{3}{5} = \dfrac{9}{25}$.

36. **C** There is only one way to get two heads, out of four possible combinations, HH, HT, TH, TT. The probability is the number of "good" outcomes divided by the number of all possible outcomes.

37. **D** Multiplying, $127,000 \times 0.09 = 11,430$. Subtracting $127,000 - 11,430 = 115,570$ residents not on farms.

38. **A** Multiplying $127,000 \times 0.17 = 21,590$ who are above the average age.

39. **C** The trials are independent, so we multiply, but the number of balls changes.

$$\frac{5}{15}(\text{reds}) \times \frac{4}{14}(\text{whites}) = \frac{20}{210} = \frac{2}{21}$$

40. **D** $(2x + 5)^2 = (2x + 5)(2x + 5) = 4x^2 + 20x + 25$

41. **–10** Since there is a greater-than-or-equal-to sign, the number –10 is part of the solution, along with all the integers from there to positive infinity.

42. $\mathbf{0.06 < 21\% < 33\frac{1}{3}\% < \frac{3}{8} < 0.47 < \frac{4}{5}}$

43. **C** Solve for y to put the equation in the slope-intercept form, $y = mx + b$:

$3x - 5y = 15 \rightarrow$
$3x - 5y - 3x = 15 - 3x \rightarrow$
$-5y = -3x + 15 \rightarrow$
$\frac{-5y}{-5} = \frac{-3x + 15}{-5} \rightarrow$
$y = \frac{3}{5}x - 3$, so $m = \frac{3}{5}$

44. **$8x + 16$**

$(2x + 13) + (6x + 3) =$
$2x + 6x + 13 + 3 =$
$8x + 16$

45. **D** This is the same as picking 4 men in a row at random.

$$\frac{6}{18} \times \frac{5}{17} \times \frac{4}{16} \times \frac{3}{15} = \frac{360}{73,440} = \frac{1}{204}$$

46.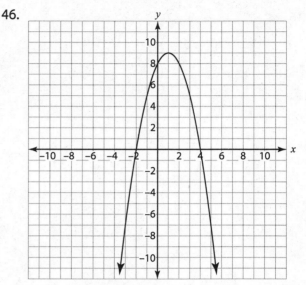

47. **C** There are six numbers on the die. The probability is the number of "good" outcomes divided by the number of all possible outcomes.

48. **A** increase $= 1500 - 1250 = 250$; percent increase $= \frac{250}{1250} = \frac{1}{5} = 20\%$

49. **$y = -7x + 21$**

The slope is $m = \frac{-7 - 7}{4 - 2} = \frac{-14}{2} = -7$. Using $y = -7x + b$ and the coordinates of the point $(2, 7)$, $7 = -7 \cdot 2 + b \rightarrow 7 = -14 + b \rightarrow 21 = b$.

50. **C** When the curve intersects the y-axis, $x = 0$. Substituting $x = 0$ results in $y = 6 \cdot 0^2 + 5 \cdot 0 - 6 = -6$.

Formulas You Need to Know

You are expected to know a few basic formulas, such as those for the perimeter and area of a square, rectangle, and triangle; the circumference and area of a circle; distance; measures of central tendency (mean, median, and mode); and total cost.

Basic Formulas

distance	$d = rt$ r = rate, t = time
total cost	total cost = unit price × number of units
measures of	mode = most frequent data value
central tendency	median = number that has half of the data values above it and half below it.
	mean = $\dfrac{x_1 + x_2 + \cdots + x_n}{n}$

Perimeter and Area

square	$p = 4s$	$A = s^2$
rectangle	$p = 2l + 2w$	$A = lw$
triangle	$p = a + b + c$	$A = \dfrac{1}{2}bh$
circle	$C = 2\pi r$	$A = \pi r^2$

(C = circumference; $\pi \approx 3.14$)

Surface Area and Volume

cube	$SA = 6s^2$	$V = s^3$
rectangular solid	$SA = 2lh + 2lw + 2hw$	$V = lwh$

(Also, see the formula for a rectangular/right prism on the next page.)

The formulas on the next page will be available when you take the GED. You do not need to memorize them, but you should become familiar with them and know what they mean and how they are used. The letter p stands for the perimeter of the base of an object; s is the length of a side of a square or cube, or the slant height of an object, depending on use; and B stands for the area of the base of a solid. Heights h that aren't slant heights must be measured perpendicular to the base. A radius is half of a diameter.

GED® Test Mathematics Formula Sheet

Area

parallelogram	$A = bh$
trapezoid	$A = \frac{1}{2}h(b_1 + b_2)$

Surface Area and Volume

rectangular/right prism	$SA = ph + 2B$	$V = Bh$
cylinder	$SA = 2\pi rh + 2\pi r^2$	$V = \pi r^2 h$
pyramid	$SA = \frac{1}{2}ps + B$	$V = \frac{1}{3}Bh$
cone	$SA = \pi rs + \pi r^2$	$V = \frac{1}{3}\pi r^2 h$
sphere	$SA = 4\pi r^2$	$V = \frac{4}{3}\pi r^3$

(p = perimeter of base B; $\pi \approx 3.14$)

Algebra

slope of a line	$m = \dfrac{y_2 - y_1}{x_2 - x_1}$
slope-intercept form of the equation of a line	$y = mx + b$
point-slope form of the equation of a line	$y - y_1 = m(x - x_1)$
standard form of a quadratic equation	$y = ax^2 + bx + c$
quadratic formula	$x = \dfrac{-b \pm \sqrt{b^2 - 4ac}}{2a}$
Pythagorean theorem	$a^2 + b^2 = c^2$
simple interest	$I = prt$

(I = interest, p = principal, r = rate, t = time)